My Art & Illustrations
Volume I

Copyright © 2020 by Jan T. Langhanki

All rights reserved. No part of this book may be reproduced or used in any manner without written permission of the copyright owner except for the use of quotations in a book review.

FIRST EDITION

Table of Contents

Minds & Matters	6
Wanderlust & Exploration	14
Flying & Falling through space	20
Paintings & Colors	26
Inktober 2020	36
Sculptures, Sketches & Scraps	50

Introduction

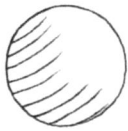

Hi! I'm Capsis and if you're reading this, you've probably heard about my art. It's almost better if you have not, because you are currently holding everything I created in 2020 in your hands. I always thought that the first book I'll publish will be a novel or a short story collection but here we are. I guess you can never really know where you'll end up. Still, art is something that I have pursued for a long time now so this book should surprise no one.

Even before this year started I was always creating things and I even took some art courses in high school way back when. Anyway I only started to draw with a more serious intent this January and I must say that I do not regret it one bit. Creating something from nothing and putting it onto paper is pure magic to me. Every part of the process I'm surprising myself and when I'm done I always feel like I have something unique that can never be recreated again in the same way. Having done this regularly for a year now, I'm happy to report that this feeling never faded.

But before diving into my art, drawings and illustrations know that they are only loosely grouped together by theme and not in any chronological order. In my opinion it is a better way to present my art in its entirety. Also a lot of my work is posted online, for anyone who wants to follow my artistic journey on a daily basis. All right, I'm not a fan of big speeches and long explanations. I think everything that needed to be said is said.
But for now have fun with my art.
I know I had a lot creating it!

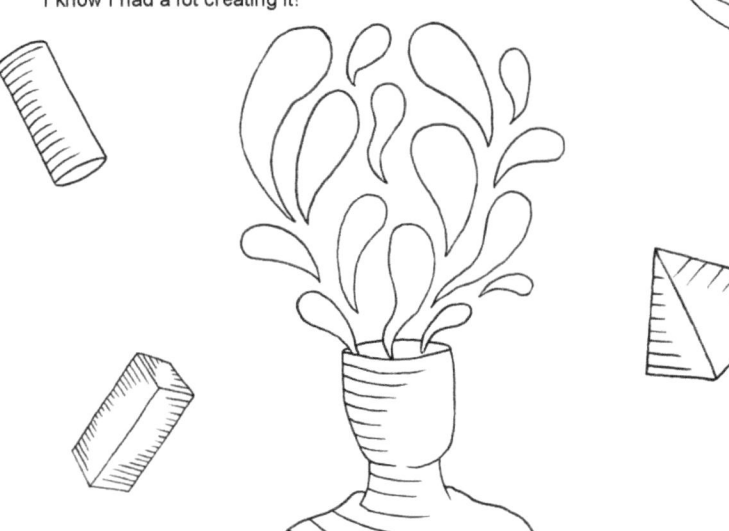

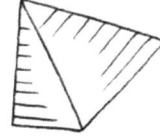

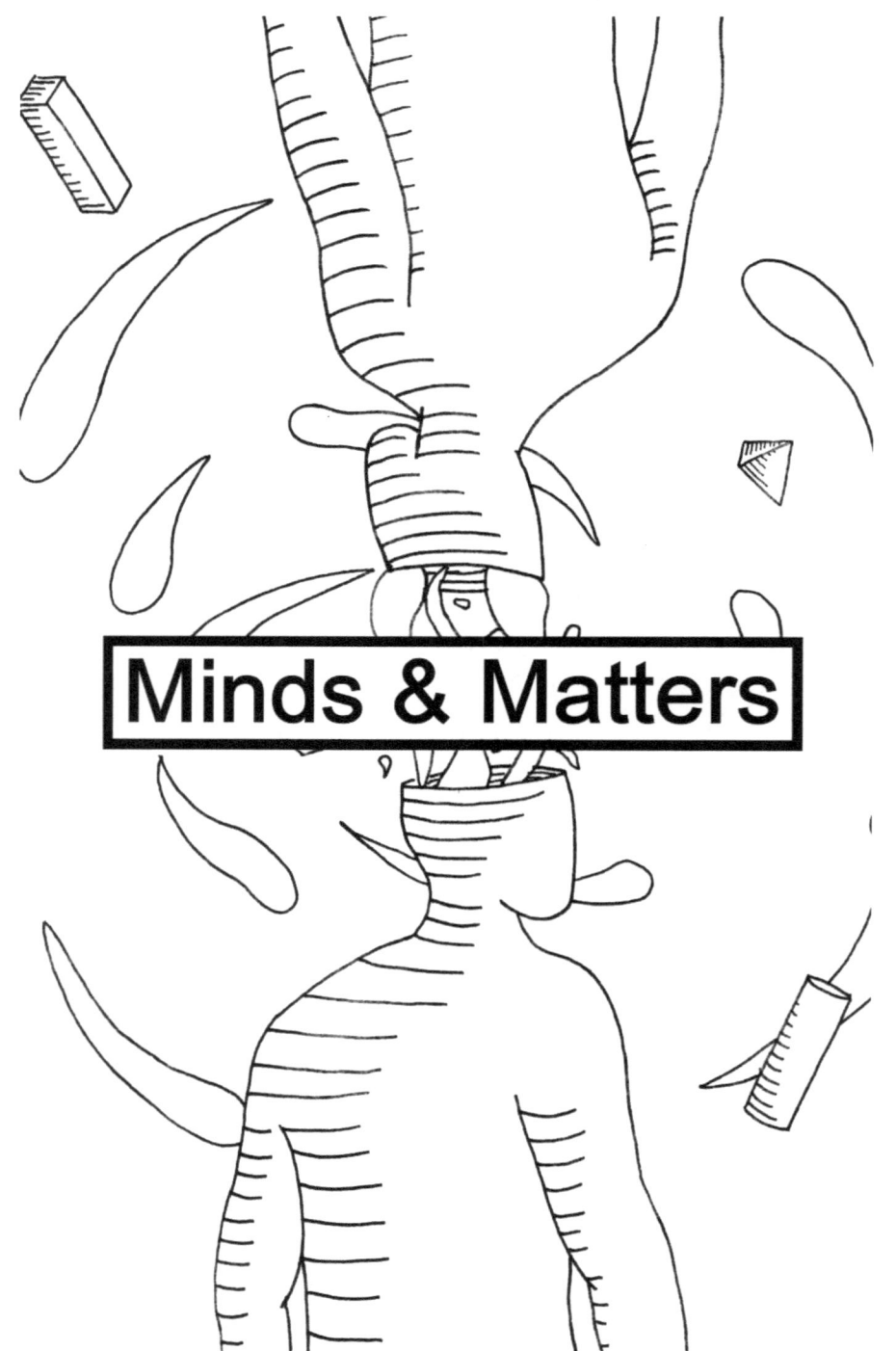

Minds & Matters

Let's start with what I consider to be my signature style (if something like this even exists). I created a lot of different things throughout the year, but these ink illustrations were the ones I probably had the most fun with.
When I finished the "Tower" on the next page it just clicked in my head. I instantly knew that this was something I wanted to explore further. And that's pretty much what I did!
I wanted to show thoughts and ideas leaving the body and I think that I did a pretty good job. If you're on the attentive side, you'll notice some reoccurring motives like the geometric shapes, stars and heads. Even though I'm the artist I don't feel like I'm the one to tell you how to interpret all these symbols.
Maybe it is not even that important. They could be seen as borders, challenges or obstacles that each of us have to overcome.
Or maybe they are just simple shapes. You decide!

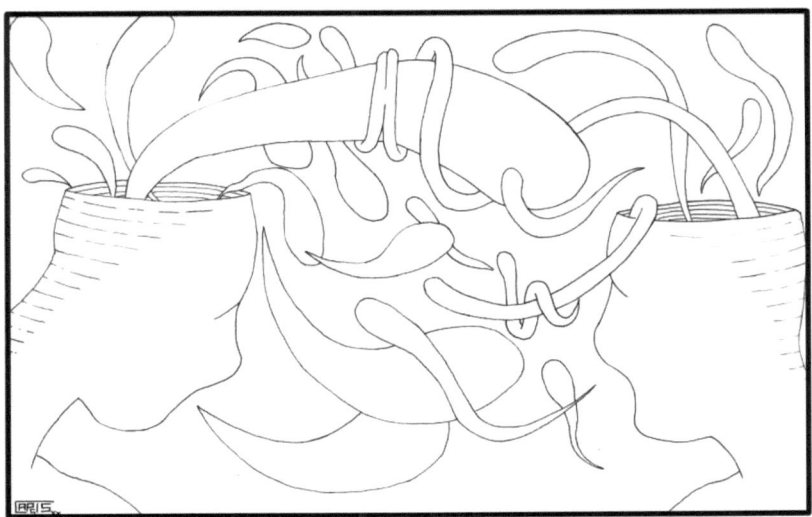

"Argument" - ink on paper

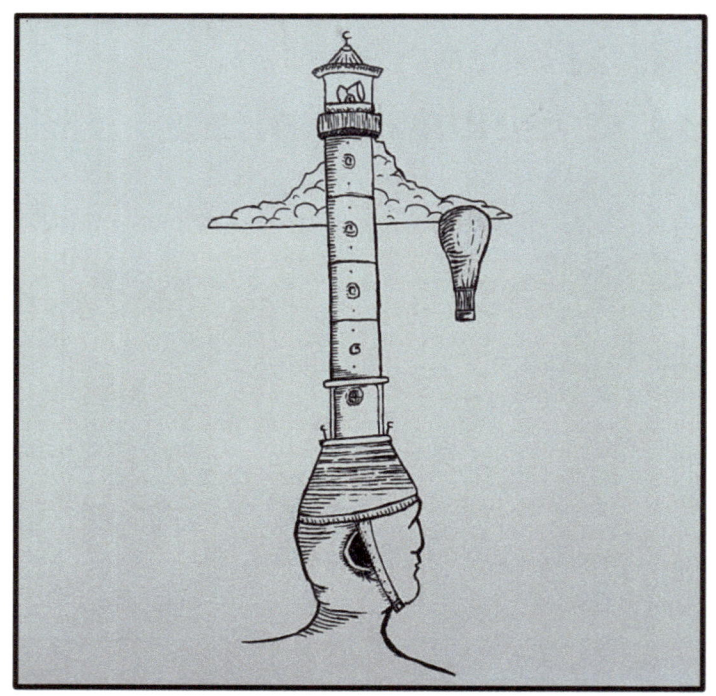
"Tower - ink on paper"

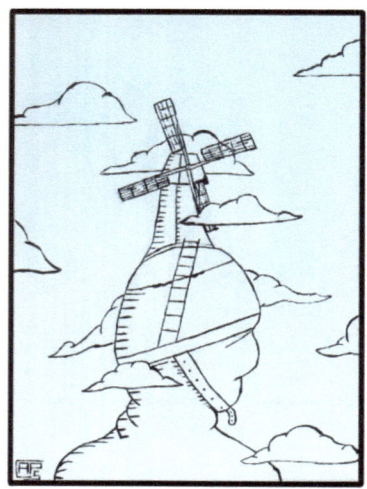
"Windmill" - acrylic paint on canvas

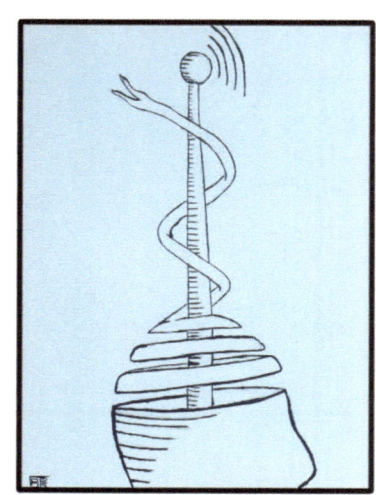
"Signal" - acrylic paint on canvas

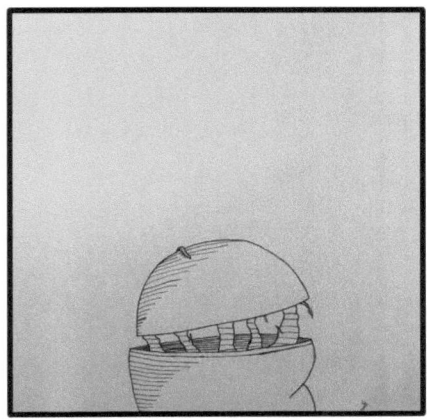

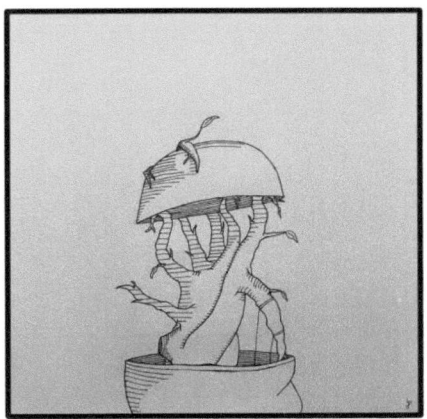

The Tree

These illustrations ("Tree 1 – 3" – ink on paper) perfectly demonstrate the beginnings of my minimalistic and surreal style.

My original intention was to create something that showed movement almost like an animation. I started working on these immediately after finishing "Tower" and I kept the elements that I felt were special. Mainly the head with something (in this case literally) growing out of it.

On the next pages you can see that this concept slowly evolved into something a bit more abstract.

The tree became more of a vessel or a placeholder for observers to put their own meaning behind. This ambiguity is almost always shown by seemingly random patterns and geometric shapes in my later works. I can't even say why, but to me it often feels like they are just supposed to be there.

Anyway this is what I consider to be my true starting point. I felt like I was slowly getting towards where I wanted to be artistically.

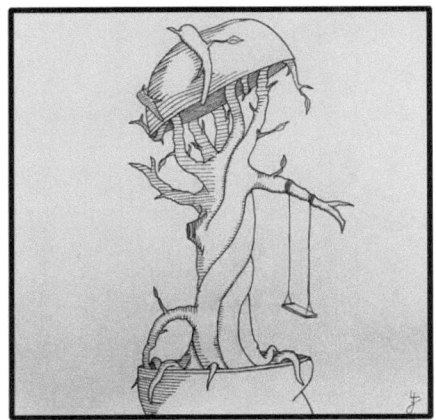

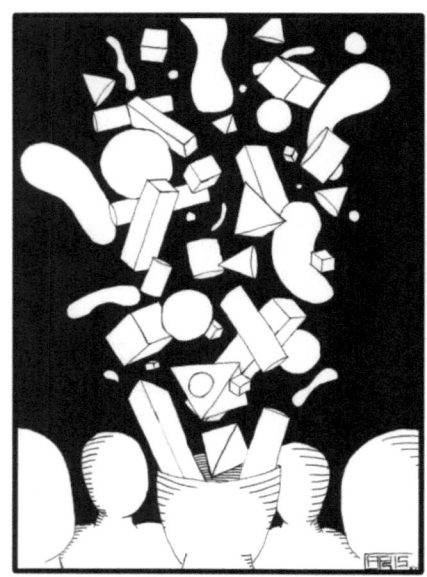
"Shapes" - ink on paper

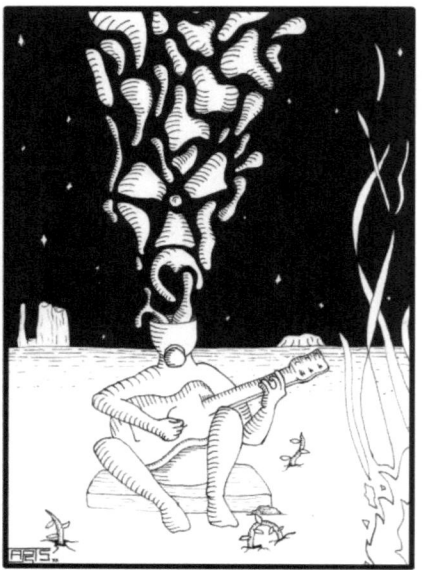
"Musician" - ink on paper

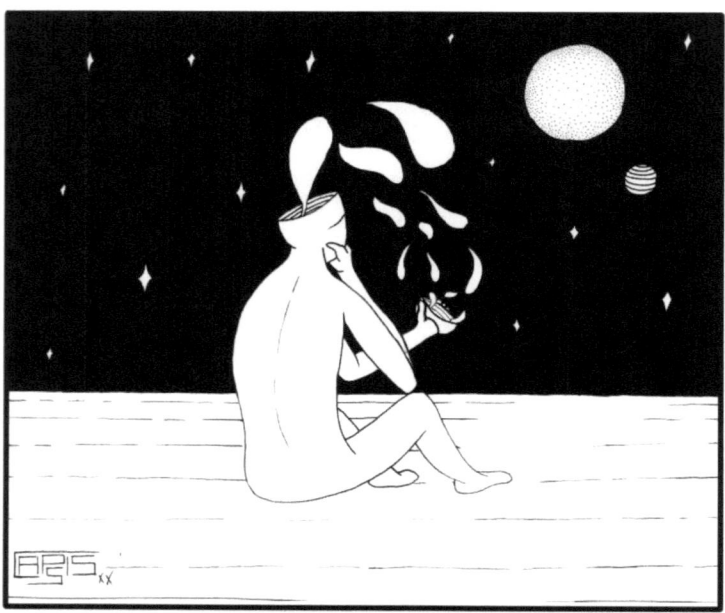
"Watching the horizon" - ink on paper

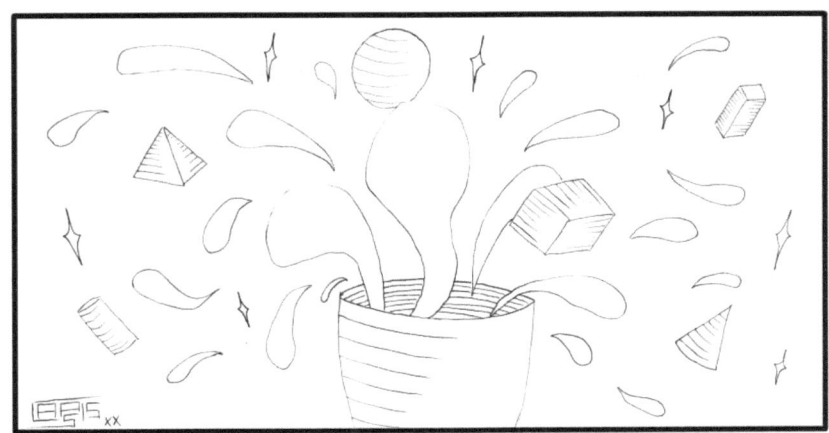
"Ideas" - ink on paper

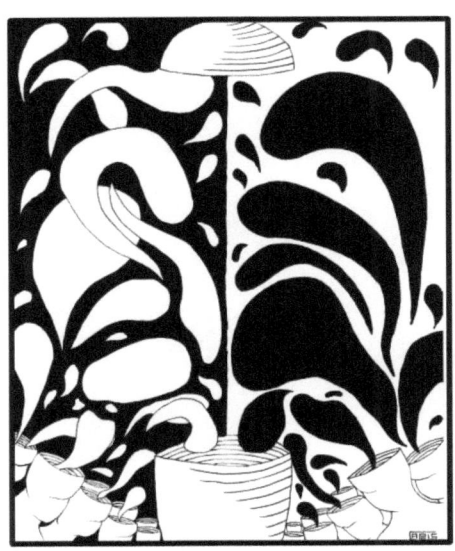
"Us vs. them" - ink on paper

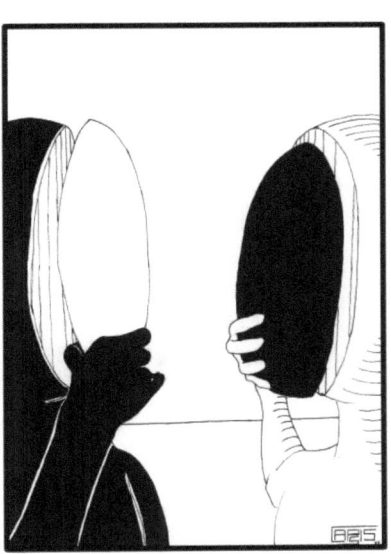
"Unmasked" - ink on paper

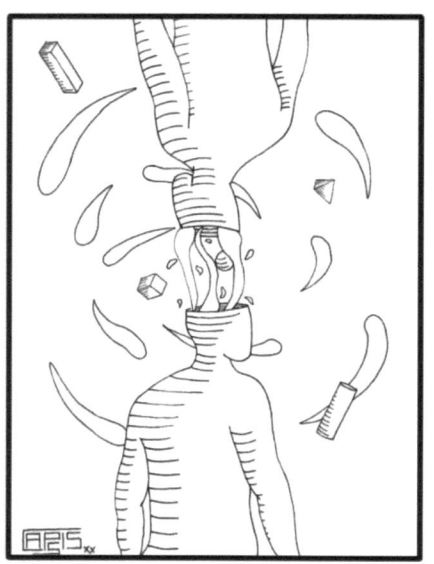
"Exchanging ideas" - ink on paper

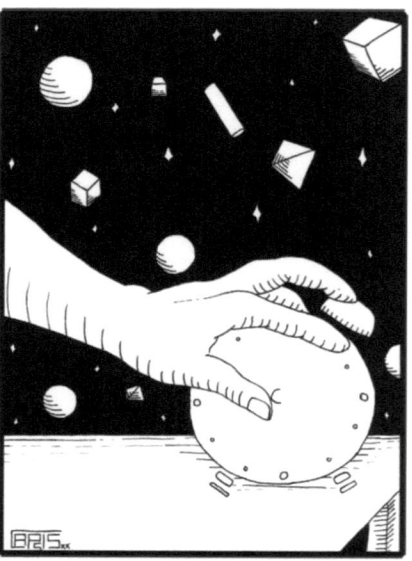
"Time and space" - ink on paper

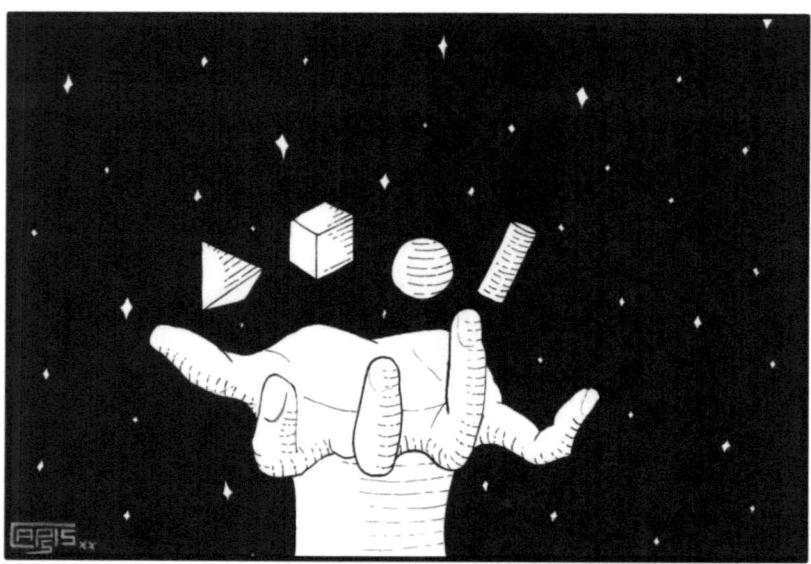
"The keys" - ink on paper

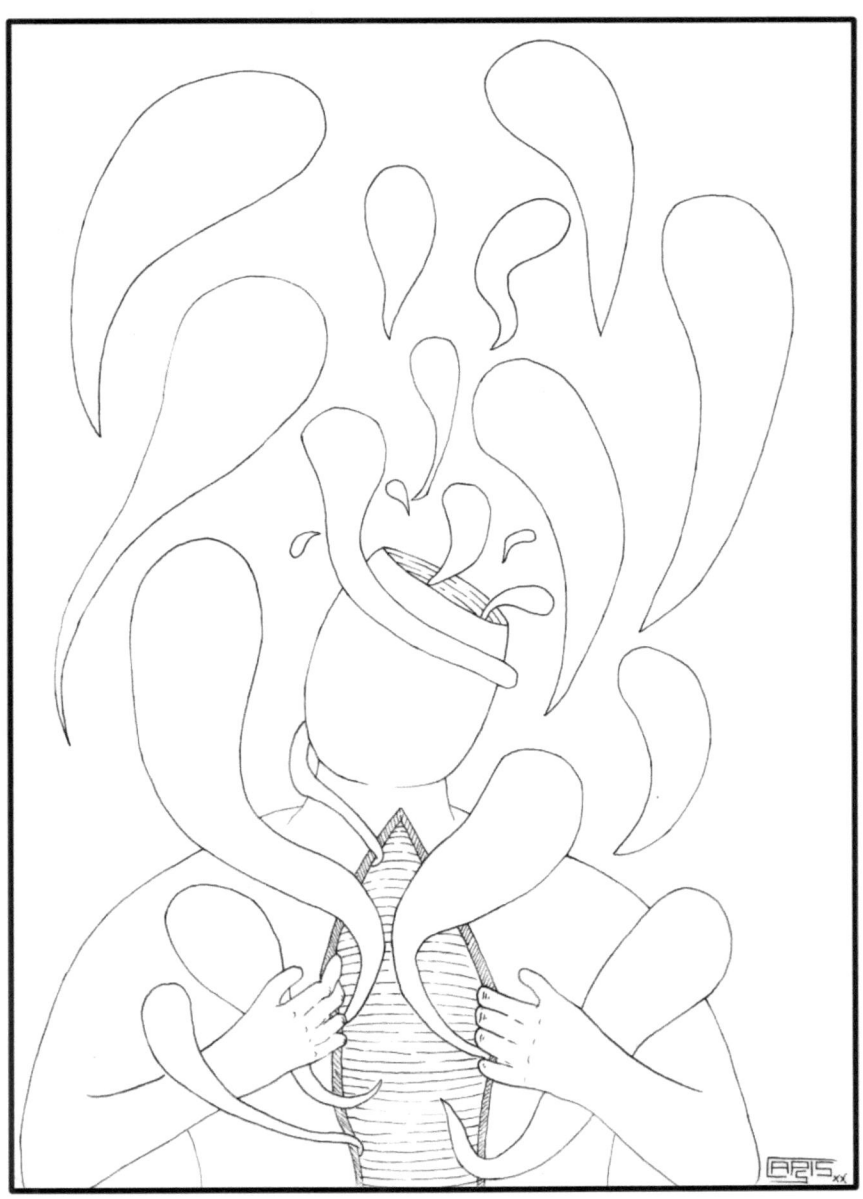

"Torn Apart" - ink on paper

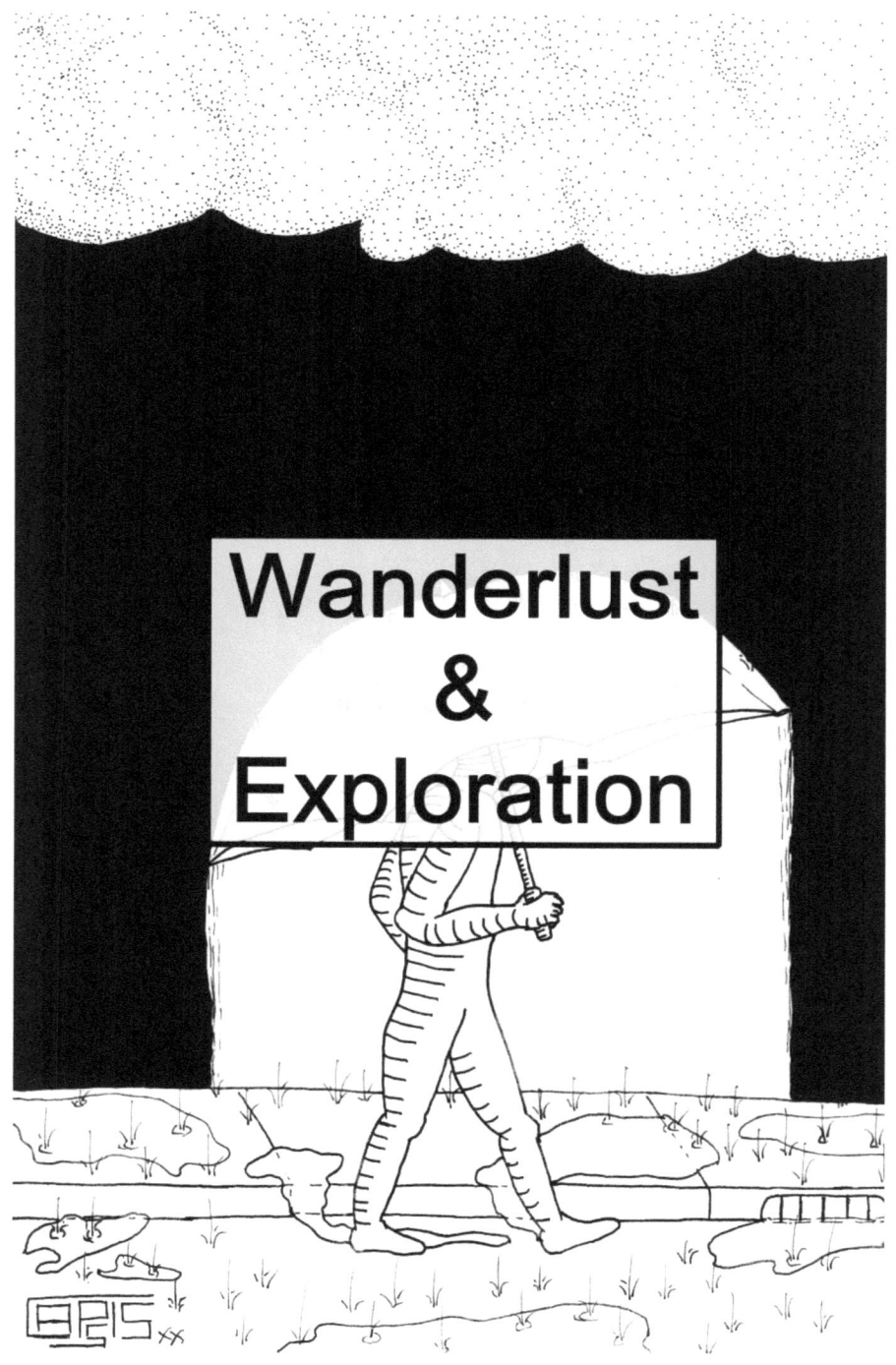

Wanderlust & Exploration

Who is up for an adventure? Just go out, leave your trusted home behind and experience all the strangeness of our world. It's something that many of us should probably do at one point.
In 2020 such endeavors have been proven to be all but impossible by strict guidelines and strange circumstances. So we have to make do with what we can imagine in our heads. Luckily that can be quite a lot. With these illustrations my goal was to capture a feeling of nostalgic exploration. Going far beyond the horizon while remaining in a dreamlike state in which your mind can travel even further.
Anyway if these words sounded interesting to you, this next chapter has a lot to offer.

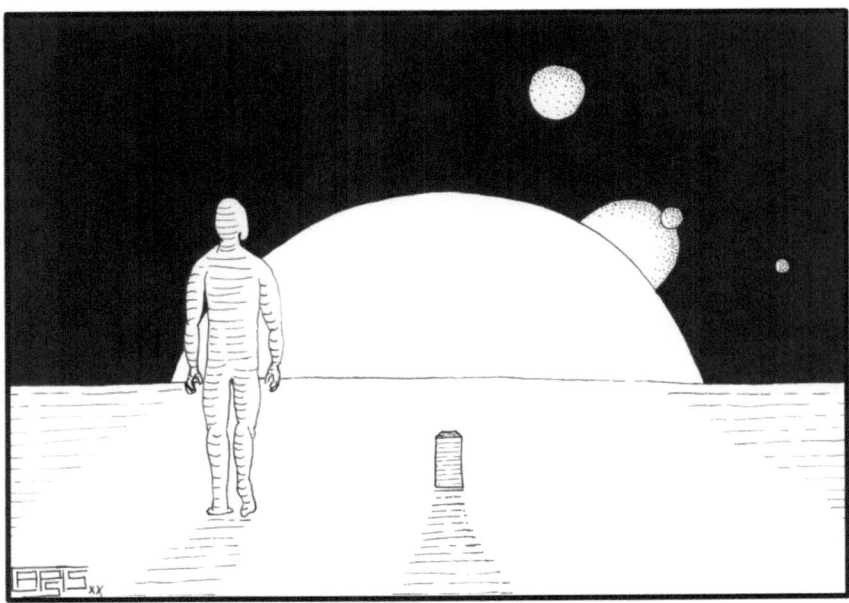

"Sunrise" - ink on paper

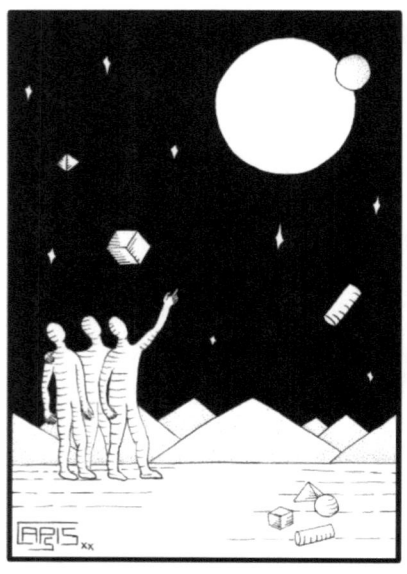

"Wanderers watching the stars"
- ink on paper

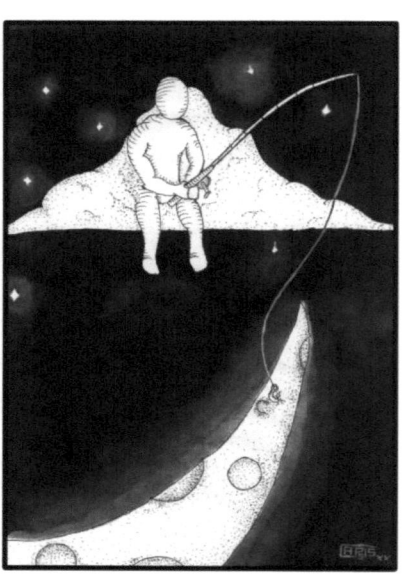

"Fishing at night" - ink on paper

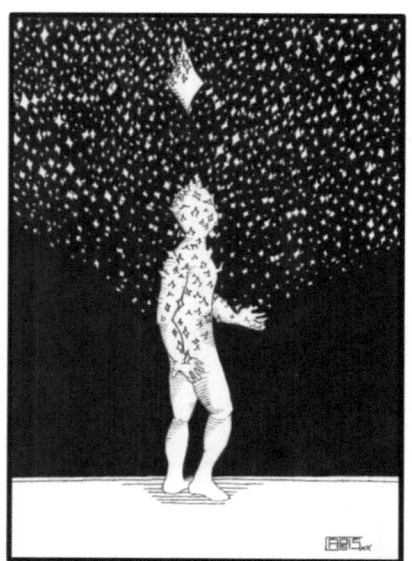

"Making of stars" - ink on paper

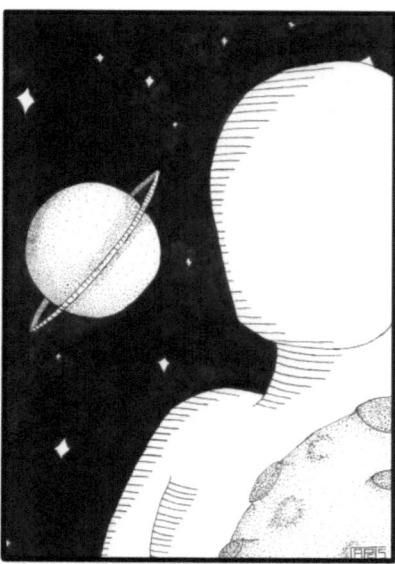

"Giant" - ink on paper

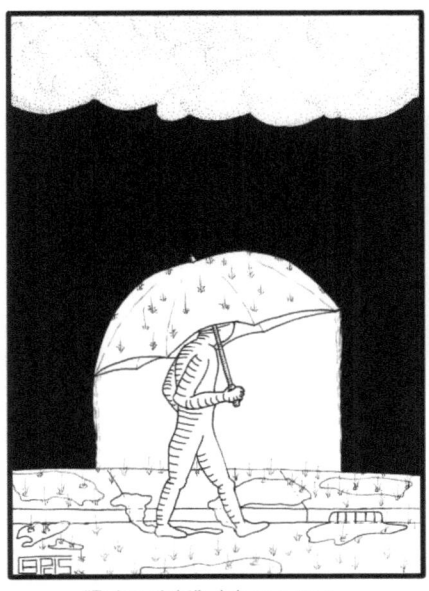
"Rainy night" - ink on paper

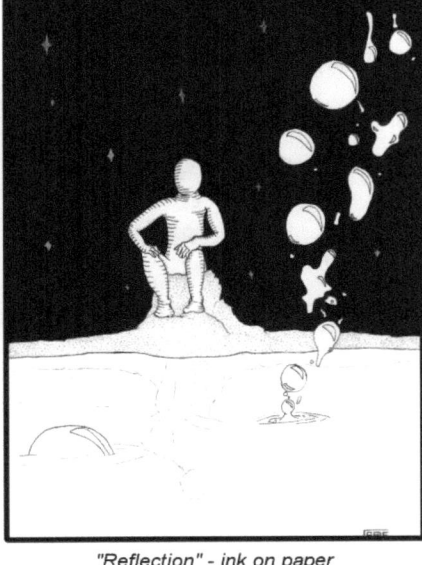
"Reflection" - ink on paper

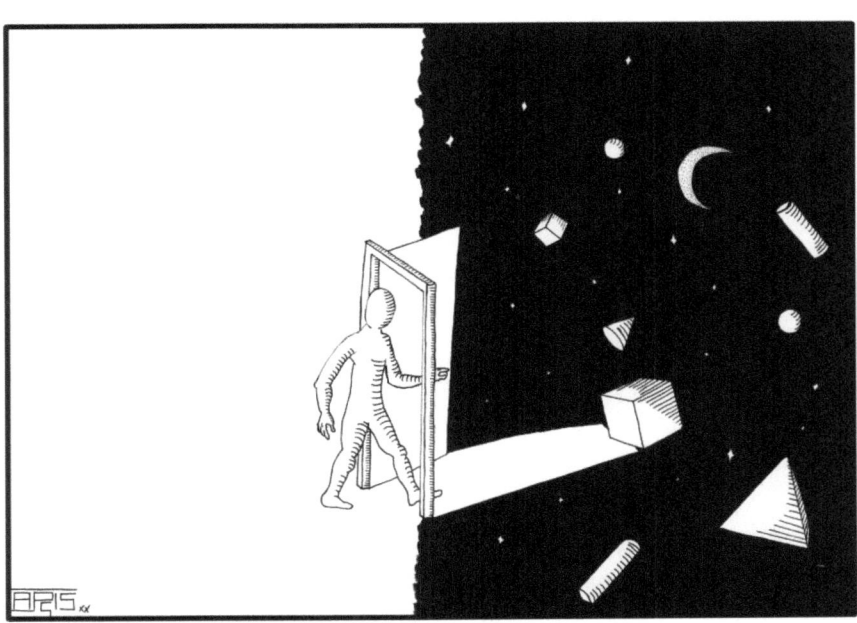
"Through the door" - ink on paper

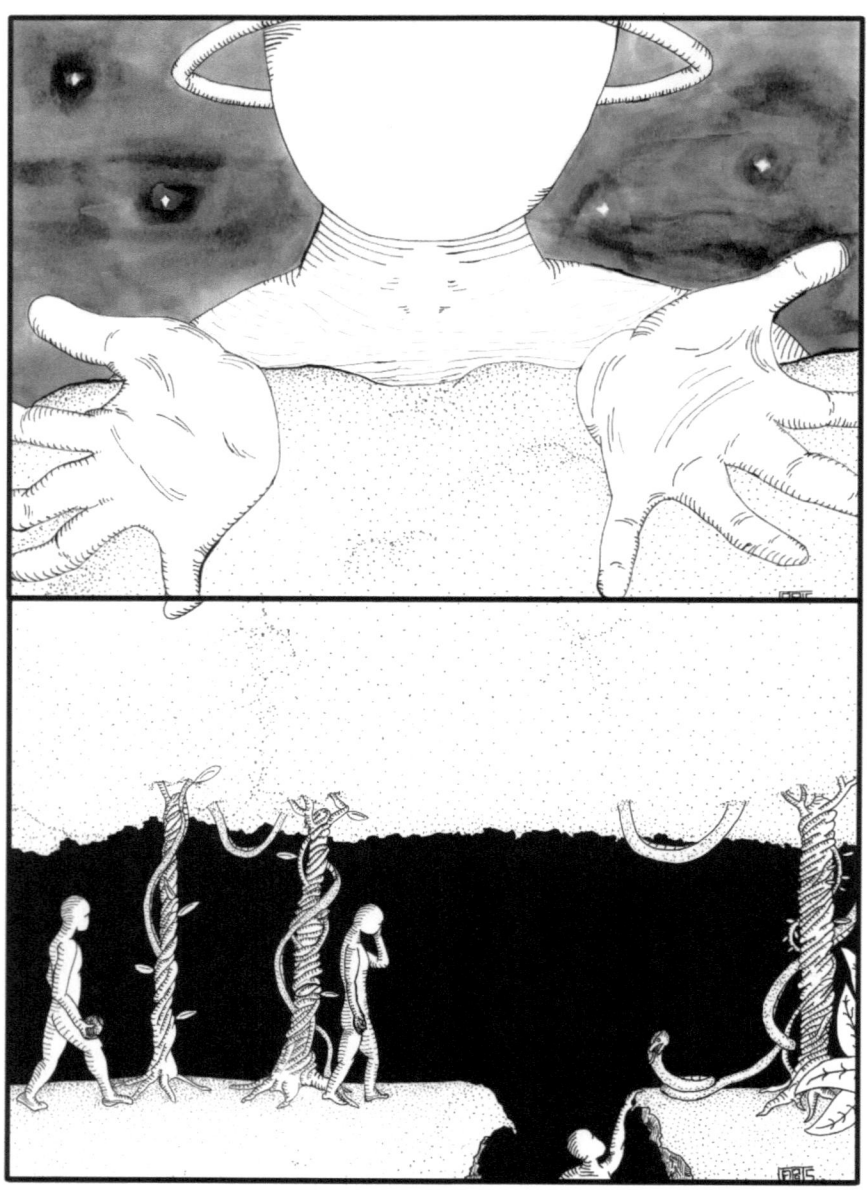

These illustrations (*"Up there"* and *"In the Garden"* - both ink on paper) are part of an incomplete series. I originally meant to create another piece below the second one but I never got around to actually doing it. But maybe I'll find some time for it in the future.

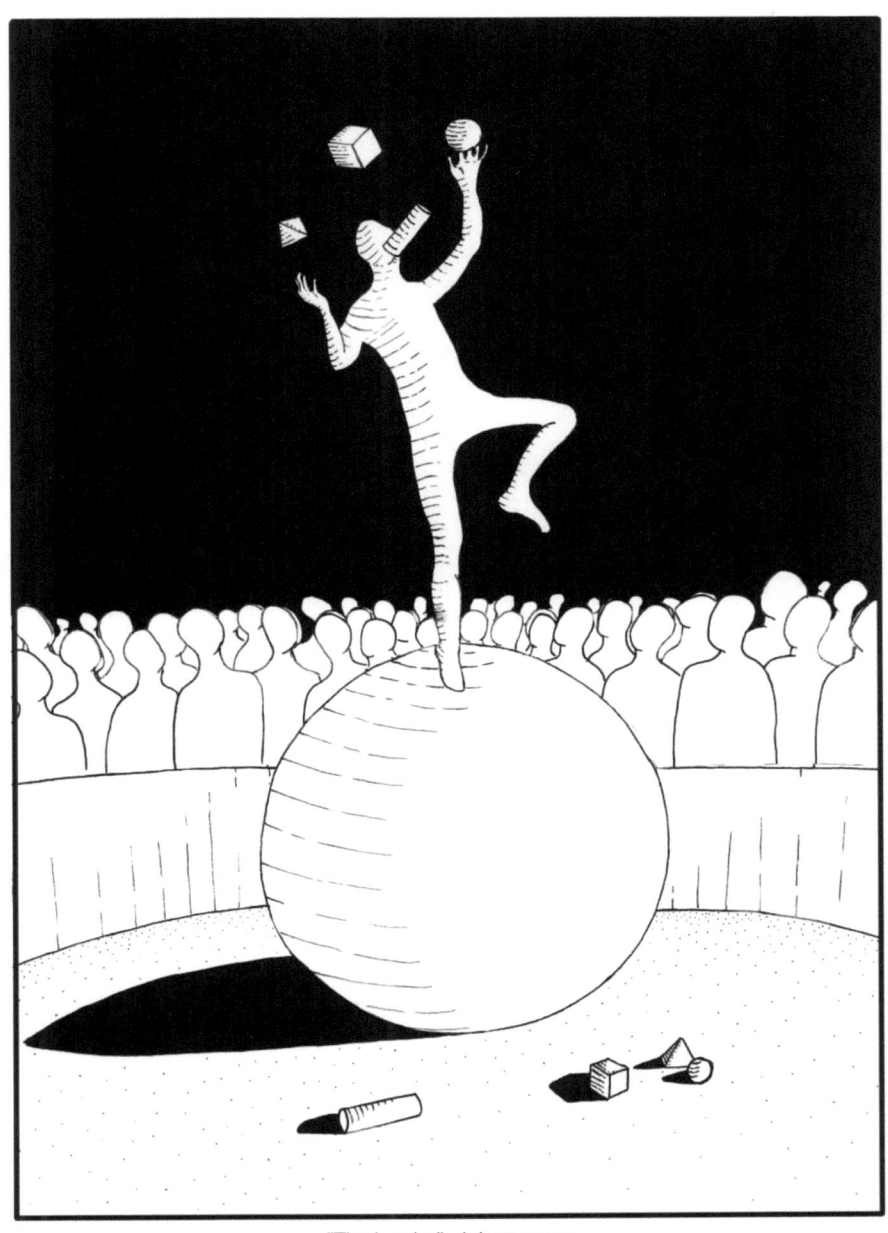
"The juggler" - ink on paper

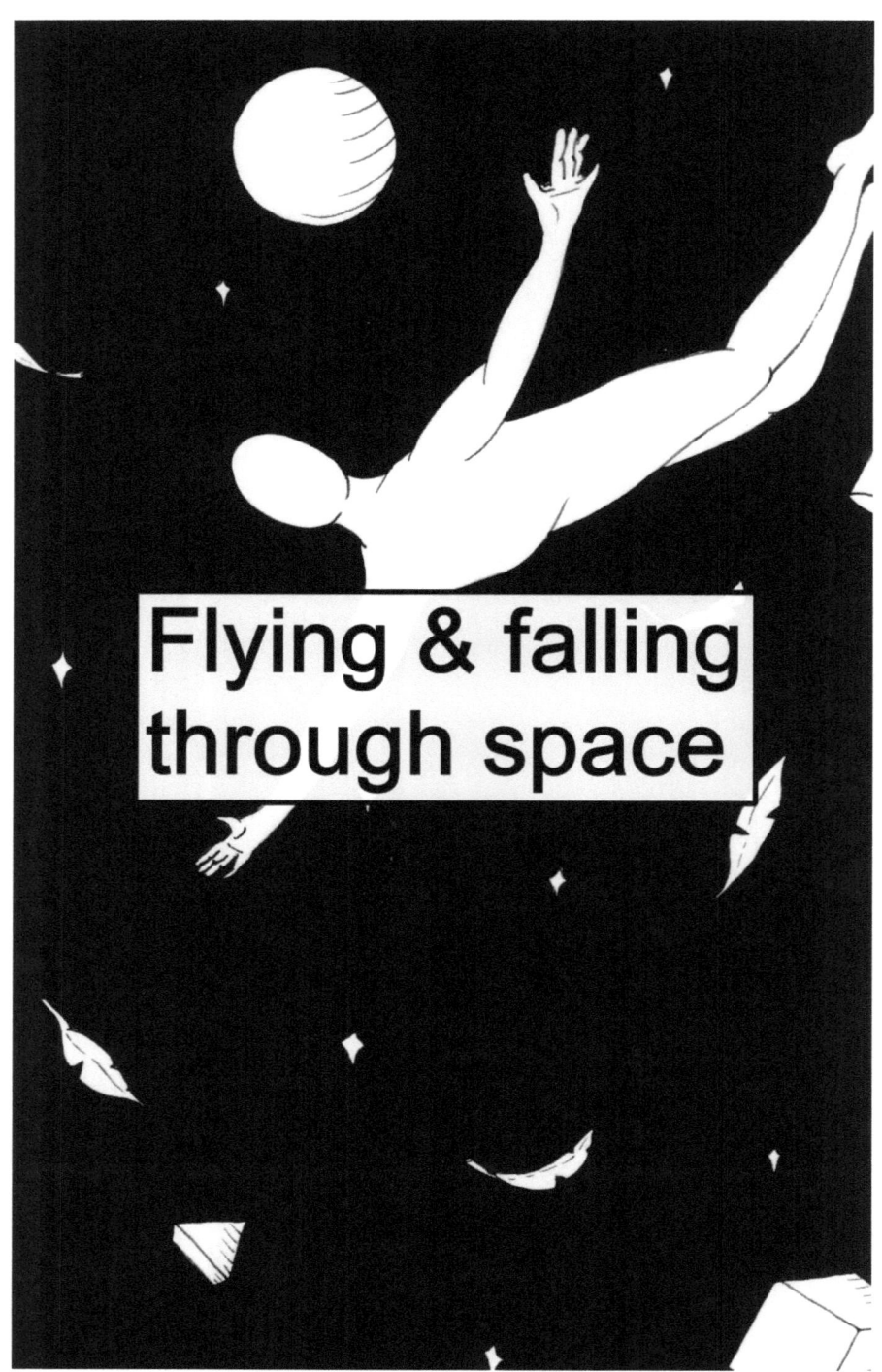

Flying & Falling through space

To me the concepts of flying and falling are fascinating. In a dream you may fly through the air, exploring every bit of the sky and enjoying infinite freedom. Soft clouds puff up right in front of you like giant lumps of cotton candy, just waiting for you to lie down on them.
But the same dream can turn into a nightmare if you lose your ability and start falling. Wind rushes by your face while the ground comes closer and ever closer. If you're lucky you awake right before impact shocked but still somewhat sleepy. Does the freedom of flying outweigh the feeling of helplessness when falling? Can one even happen without the other? How can it be that so many people have similar dreams about flying and falling?
Maybe I'm just overthinking things. I just noticed that a lot of my characters were flying or falling in my illustrations, so I went ahead and gave them their own little chapter in this book.

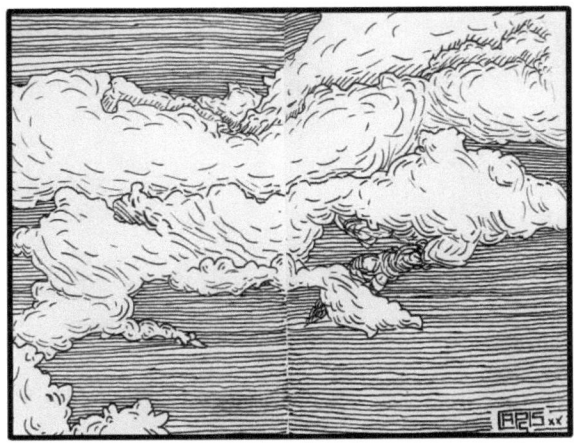

"Clouds" - ink on paper (sketchbook)

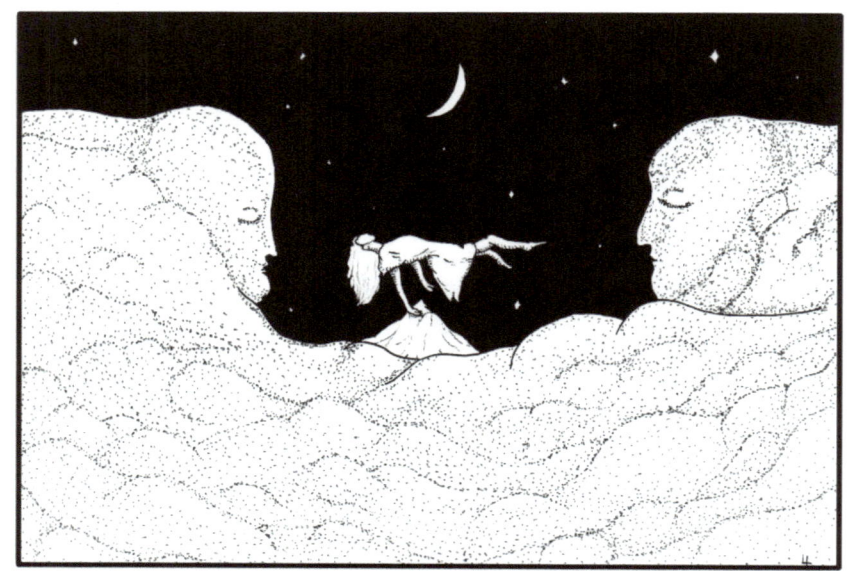
"Sleep" - ink on paper

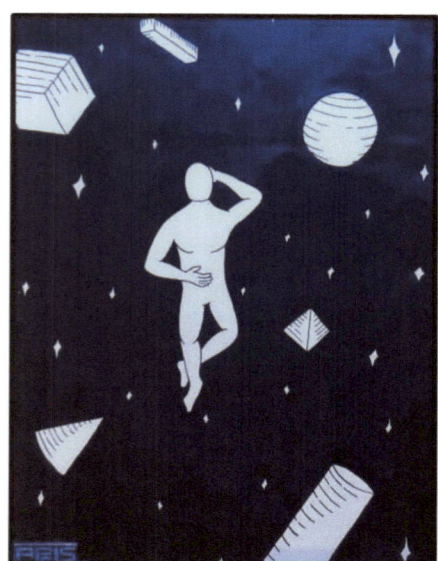
"Relaxing" - ink on paper

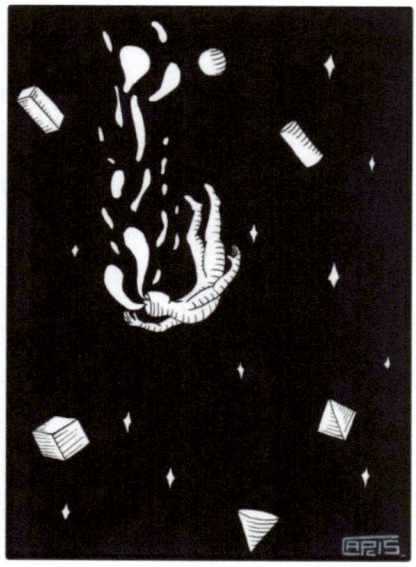
"Falling II" - ink on paper

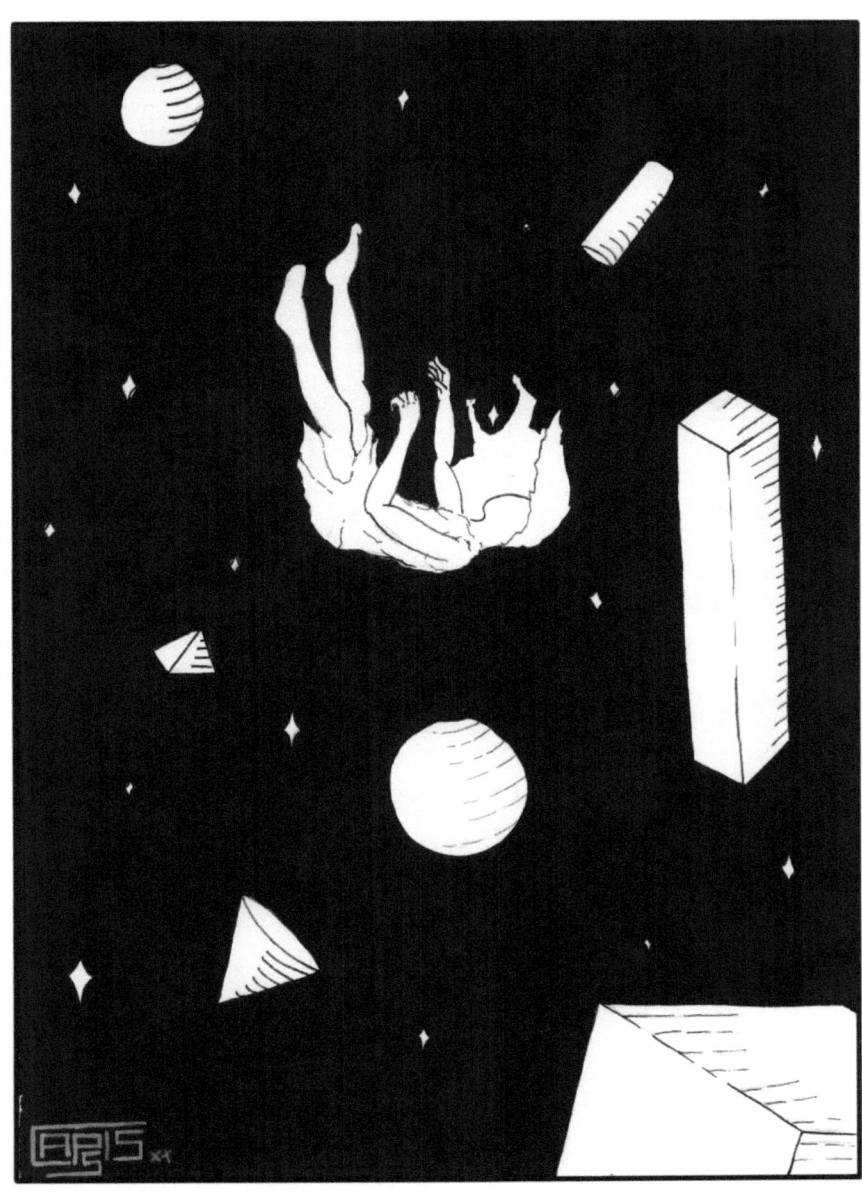
"Falling" - ink on paper

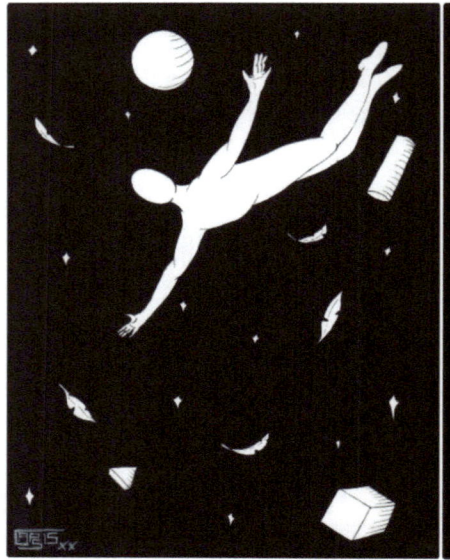

"Flying through space" - ink on paper

"Search for nature" - ink on paper

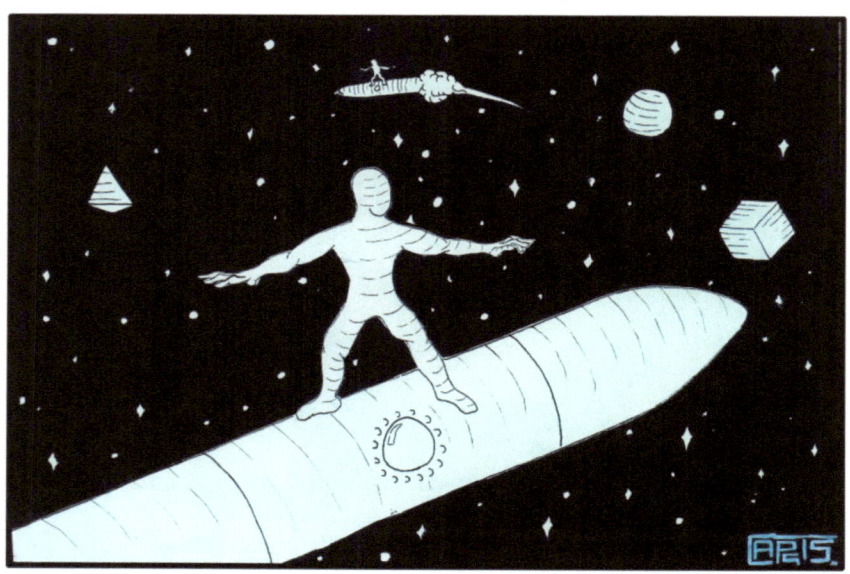

"Rocket riders" - ink on paper

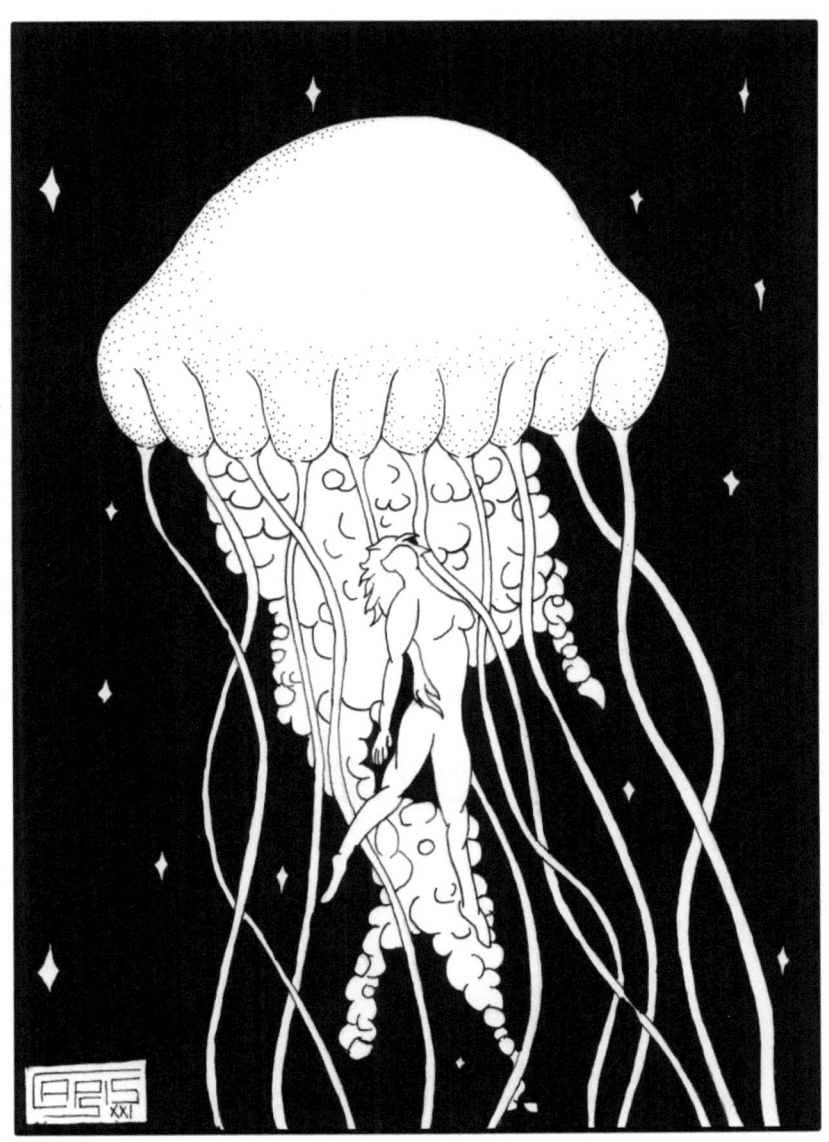
"Jellyfish" - Ink on paper

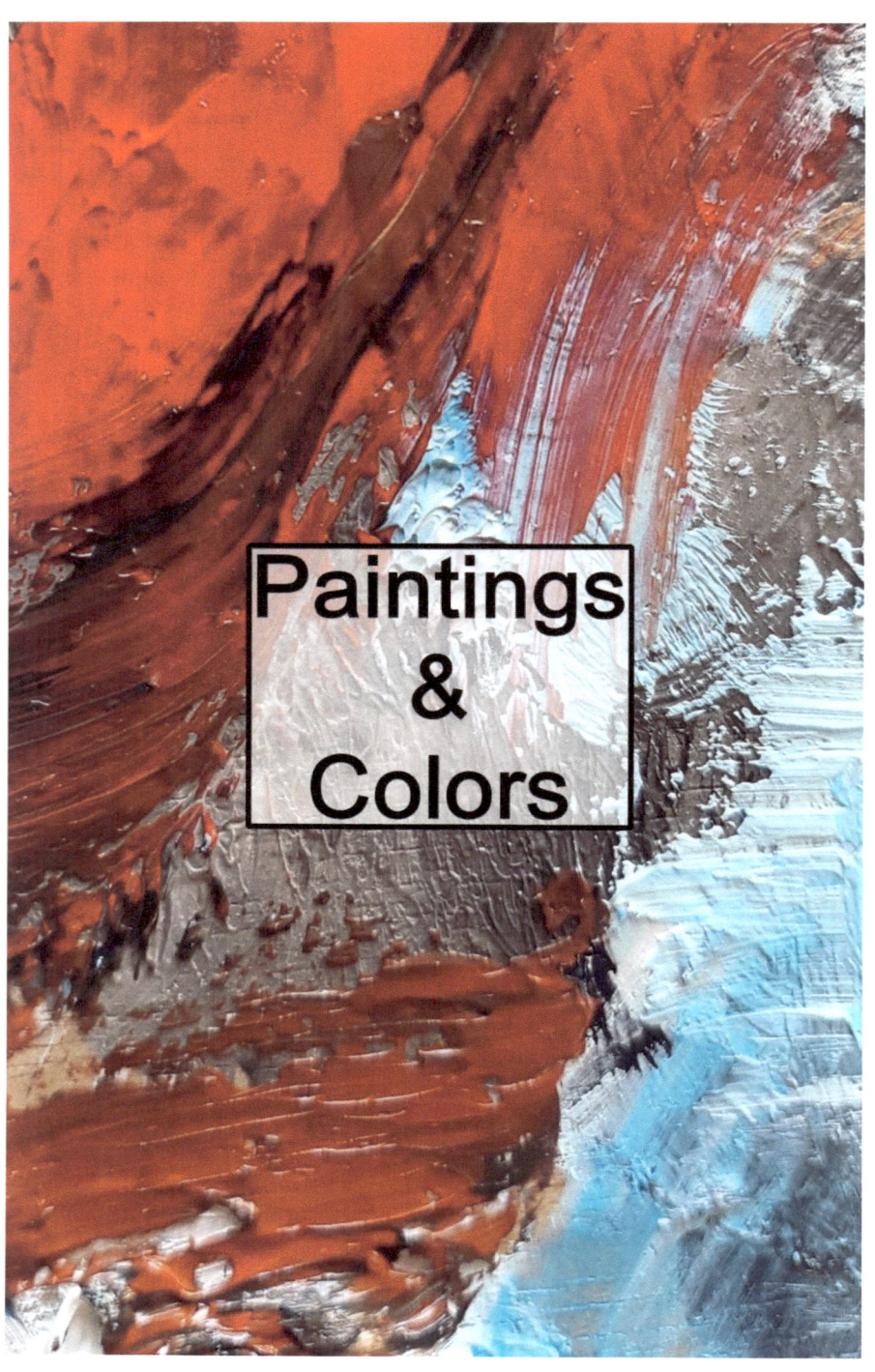

Paintings & Colors

Color is such an important tool in any artist's arsenal and this year I used it somewhat sparingly. Nevertheless, I created some paintings and colored drawings that I am really proud of. It is obvious that they differ drastically from the more illustrative style of the previous chapters.
Most of my paintings are what a majority of observers would probably consider to be abstractions of reality, while others seem to be more realistic. It feels like I completely change my approach on a subject every time I use a new medium, whether its acrylic paint, oil colors or Gouache (something I've never even heard of before this year).
Maybe it's best if you just see for yourself...

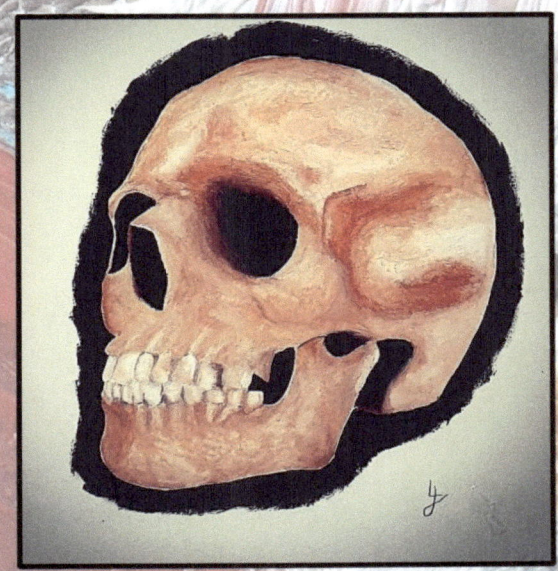

"Skull" - Oil paint on paper

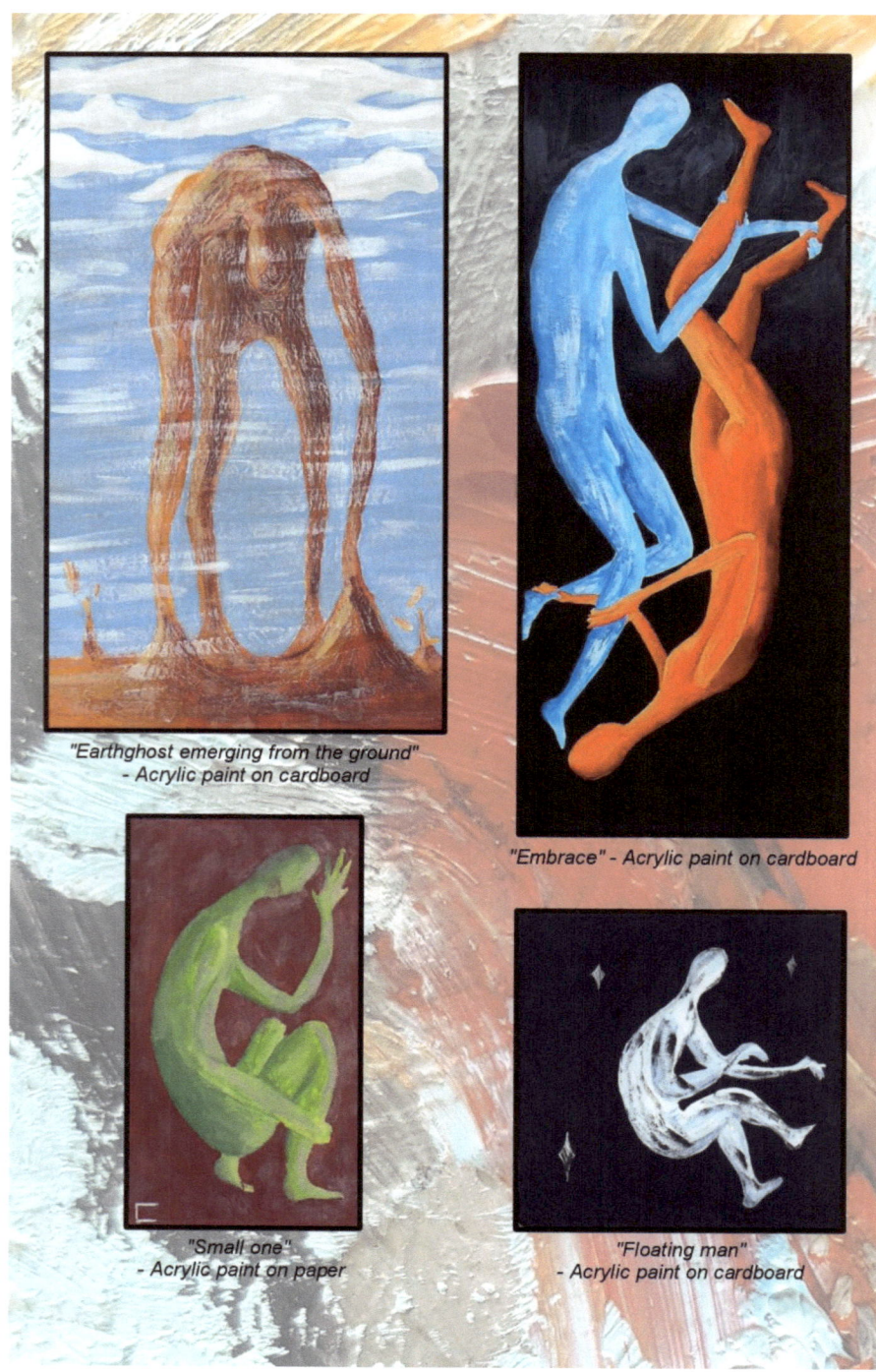

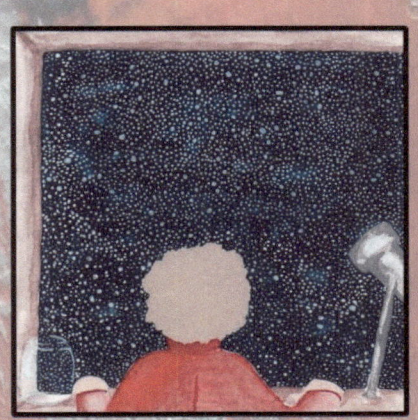
"Stargazing" - Gouache

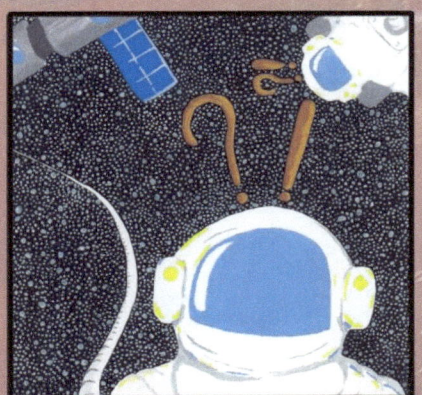
"Astronauts" - Gouache

Painting a Story

I created all of these paintings for a storybook I'm currently still working on. Gouache, the medium I used is very interesting. It somehow behaves like watercolor and acrylic paint at the same time and allowed me to take more of an illustrative than a painterly approach (If that makes sense).
Anyway, painting something based on a story proved to be quite a challenge, when I initially started but now that I'm slowly seeing how everything fits together I'm growing quite confident.
If these look interesting to you look out for "I Wish Upon A Shooting Star", which will be published at some point in 2021.

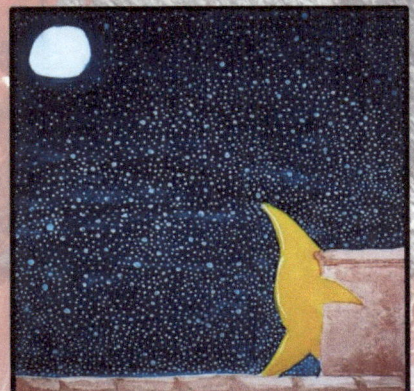
"There's a star hiding on the roof" - Gouache

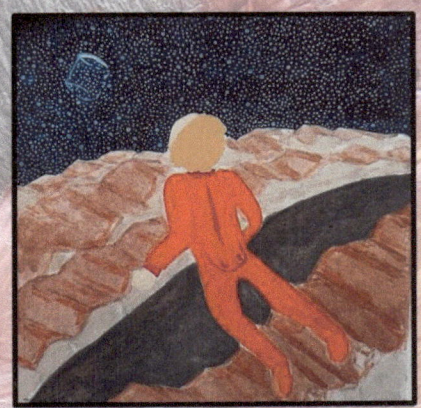
"Going up" - Gouache

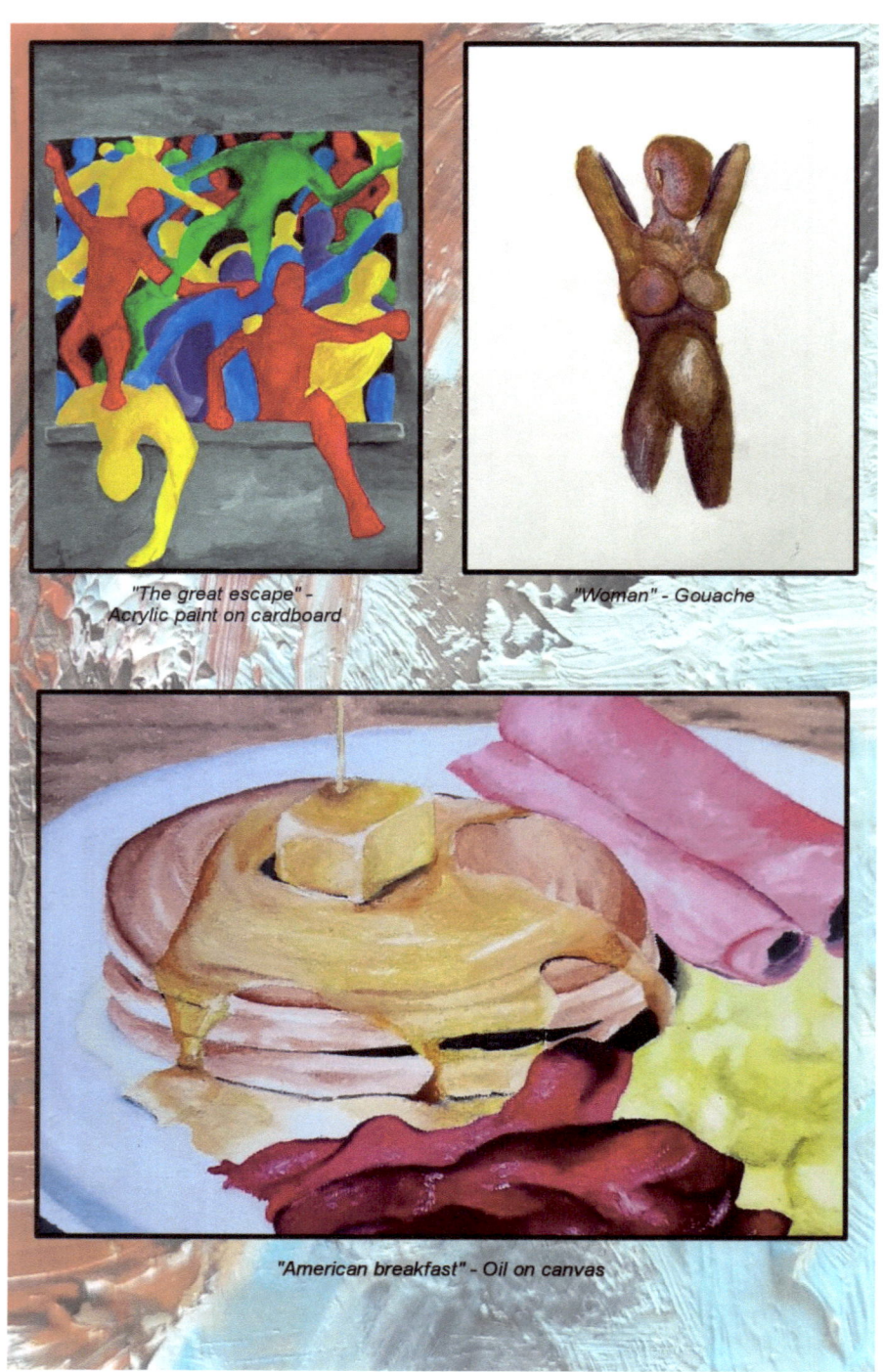

"The great escape" - Acrylic paint on cardboard

"Woman" - Gouache

"American breakfast" - Oil on canvas

Progress Report

I think there are few things more satisfying than watching a painting progress through different stages until it is complete.
On the next pages I'll show you exactly that on two of my favorites. Maybe it will give you an insight on my creative process. At the very least it should be interesting to see my approach on working with oil on canvas.

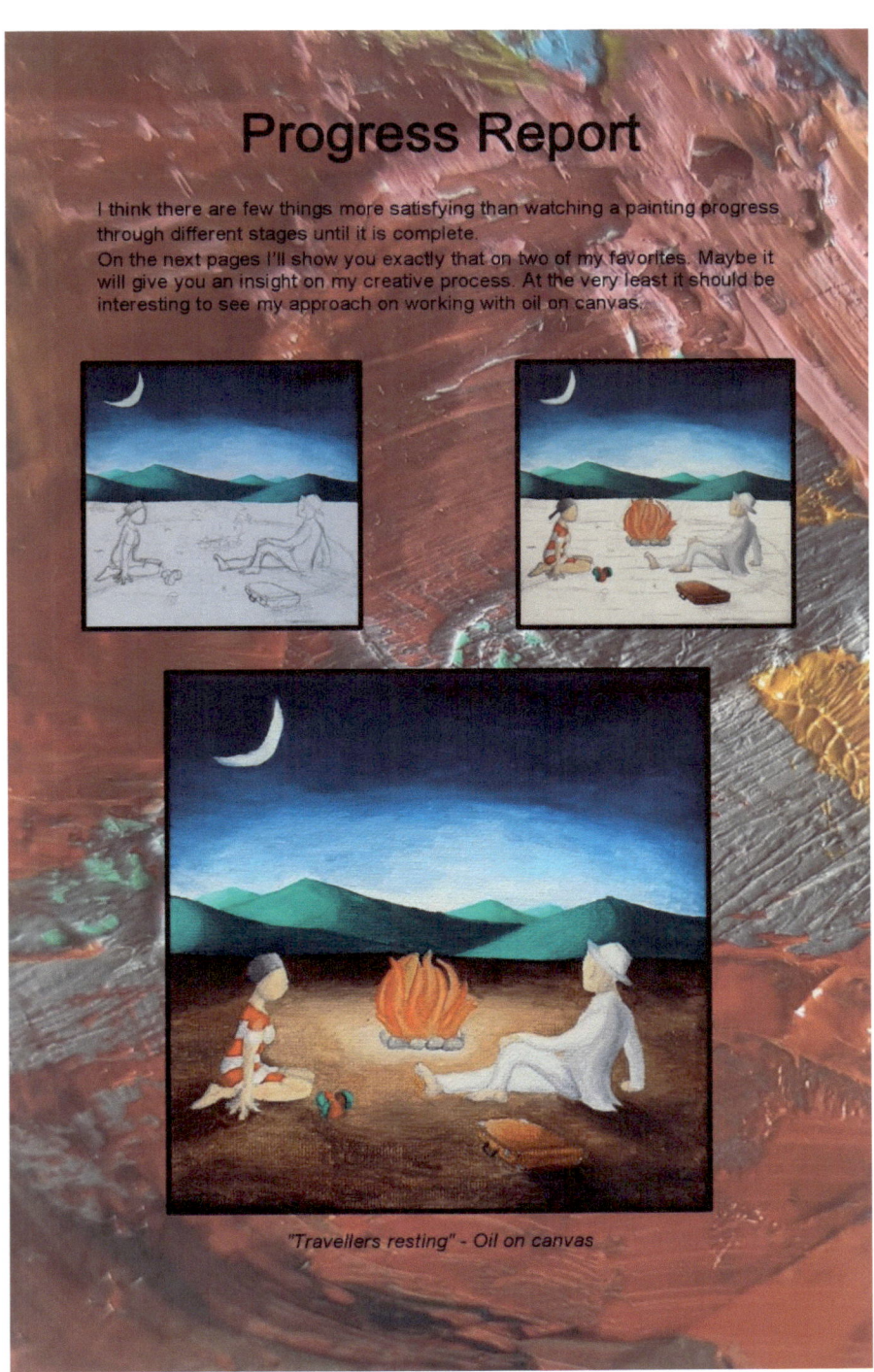

"Travellers resting" - Oil on canvas

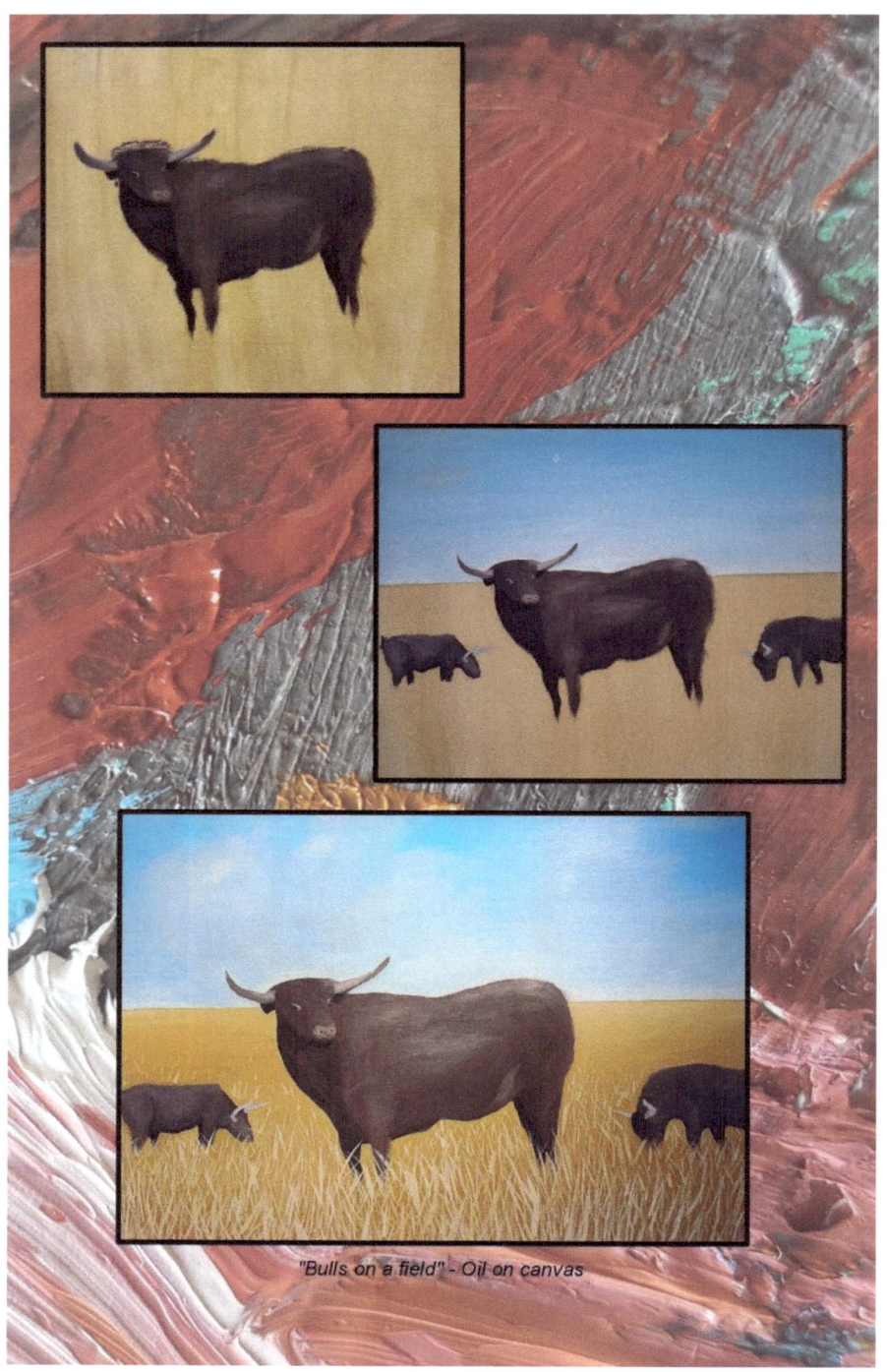
"Bulls on a field" - Oil on canvas

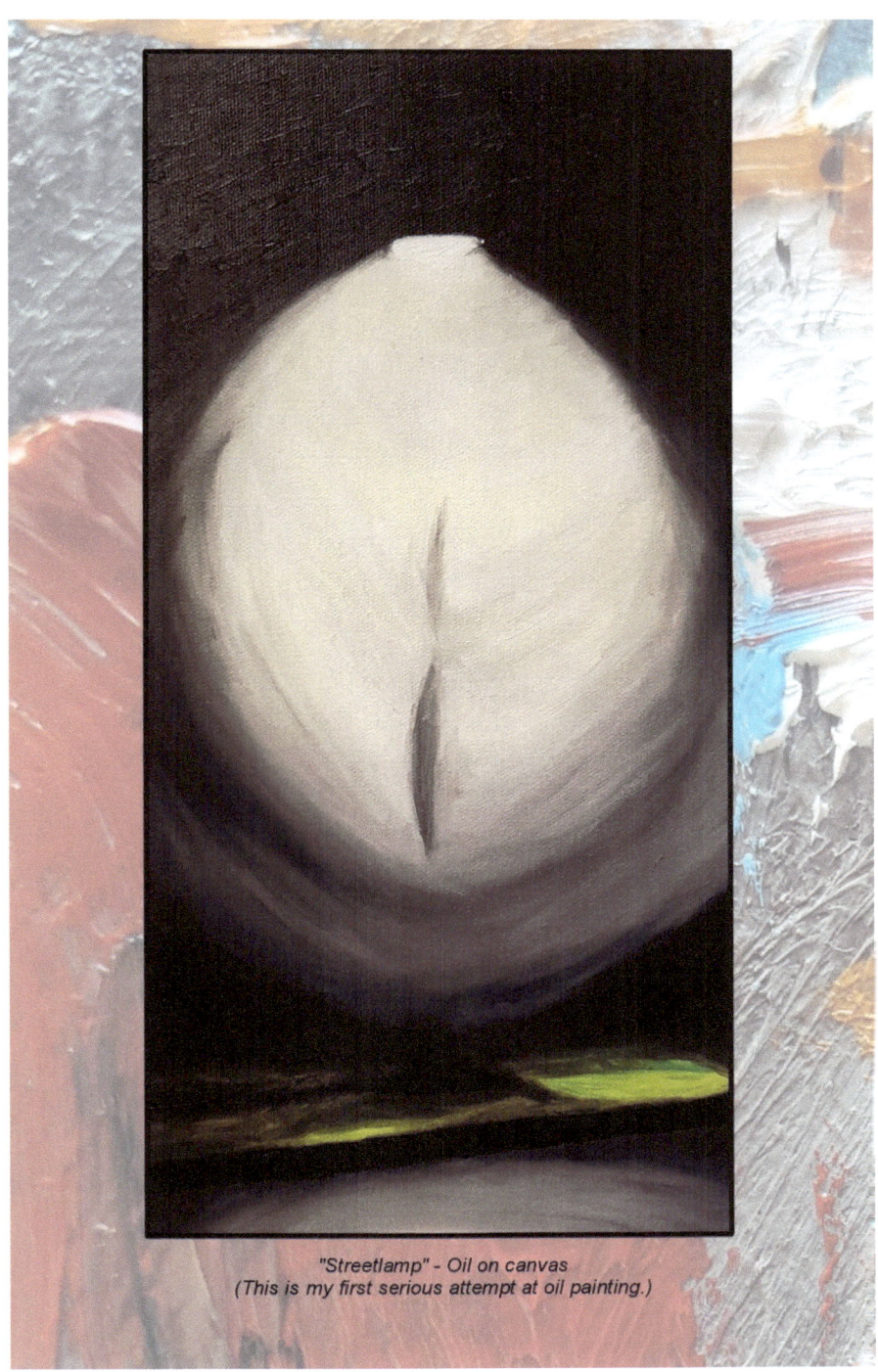

"Streetlamp" - Oil on canvas
(This is my first serious attempt at oil painting.)

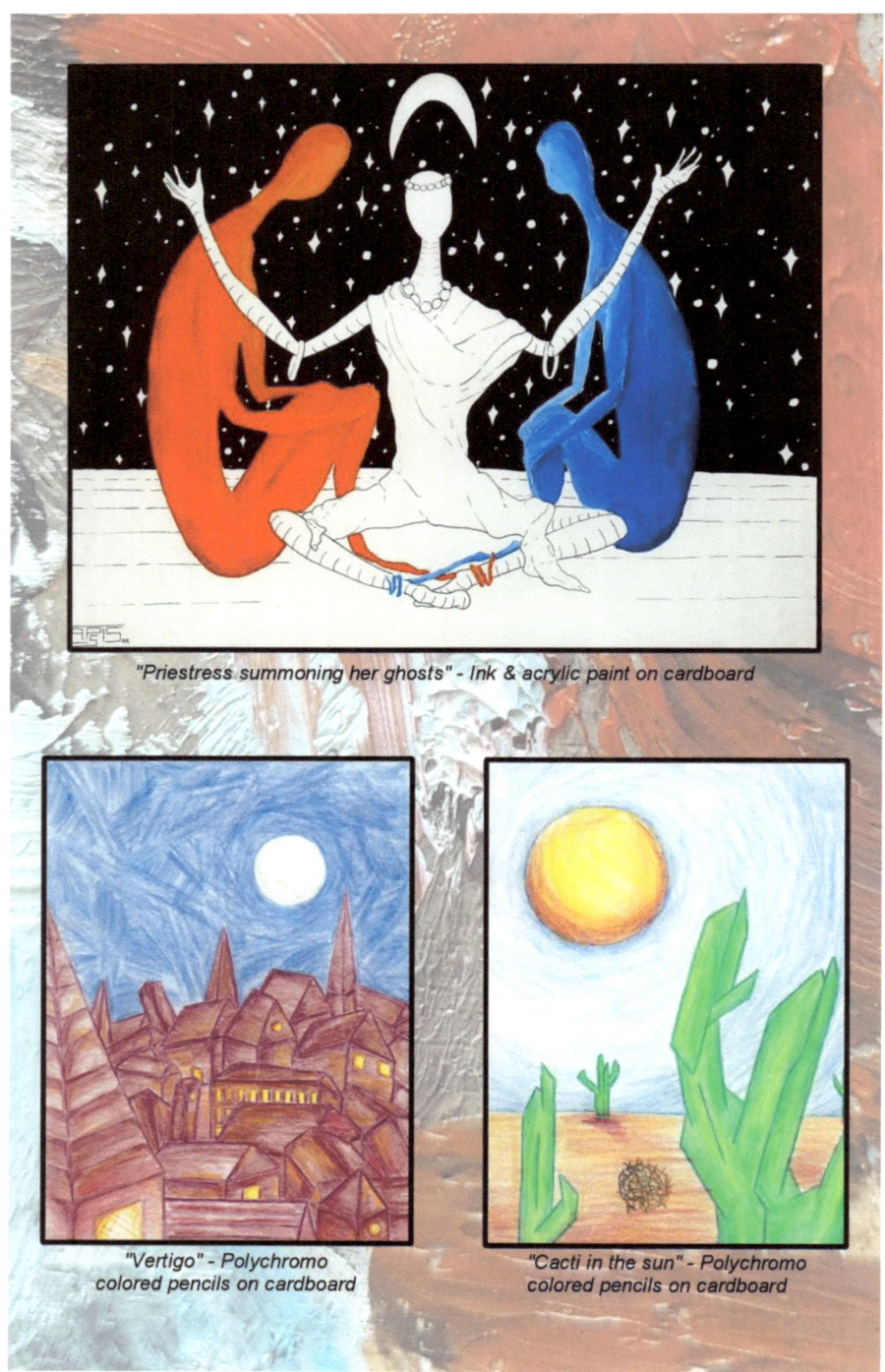

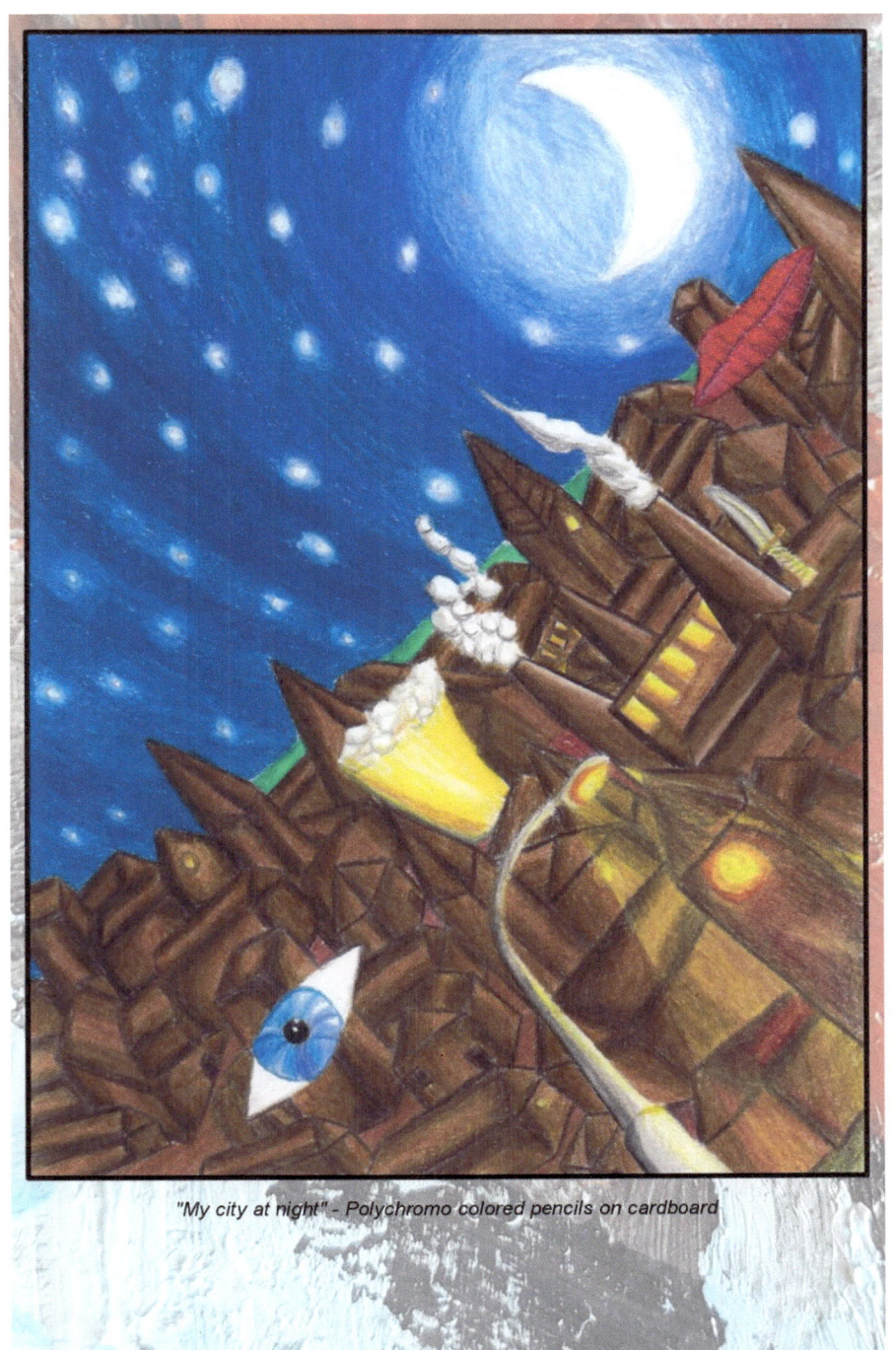

"My city at night" - Polychromo colored pencils on cardboard

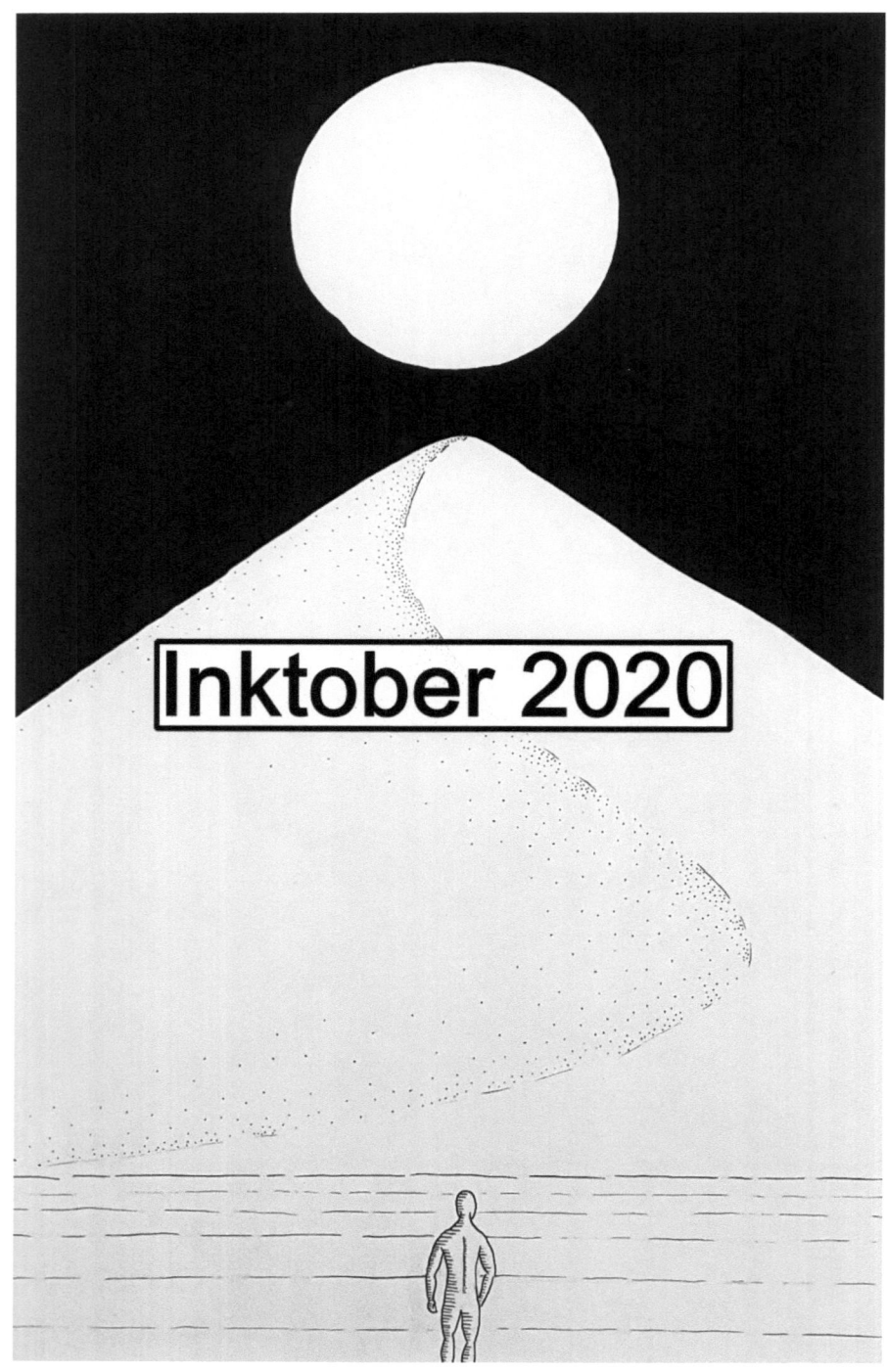

Inktober 2020

Artistically speaking 2020 was a year of firsts for me. My first ink illustration, my first oil painting, my first sculpture...The list goes on. However what I am most proud of is my first art challenge I fully completed. Let me try to briefly explain the idea behind the Inktober challenge for anyone who doesn't already know.

A list of 31 prompts is posted online and artists around the world are challenged to share one finished ink related artwork every day in October (hence the name). When I stumbled upon this challenge I just started to realize how much I loved working with ink, so the timing was impeccable.

Creating a full illustration a day, 31 days in a row proved to be quite difficult. I can't tell you how, but I managed to post every drawing on time without exception.

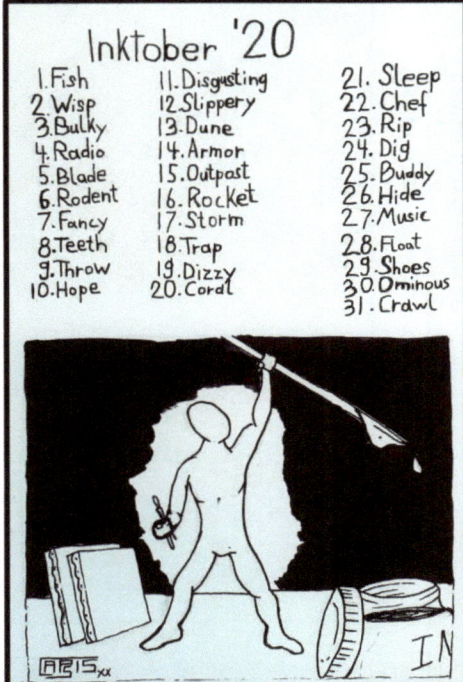

The feeling of finishing that last prompt on time is hard to explain. I felt like the person in the illustration, exhausted but happy at the same time. Probably the same feelings you'll have after finishing a marathon (although I can't confirm that theory).

Alright, here is what I came up with for the Inktober challenge 2020. Just remember I had less than a day to create each of these.

Here is a list of every prompt for this year. I don't think I need to say this but all of the illustrations in this chapter are created with ink on paper.
They were done in a little sketchbook I bought just for this purpose.

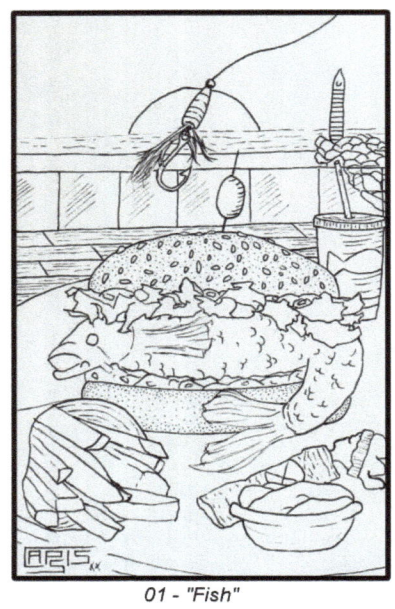
01 - "Fish"

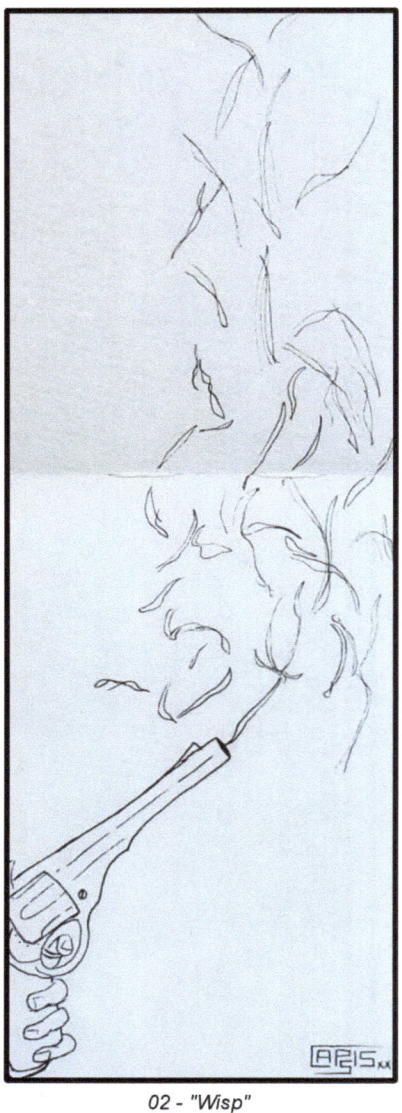
02 - "Wisp"

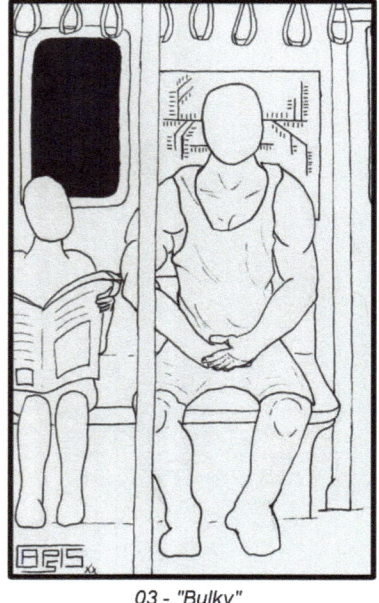
03 - "Bulky"

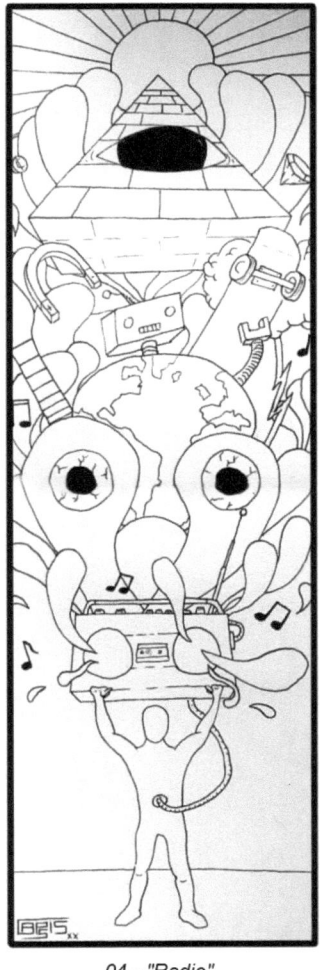
04 - "Radio"

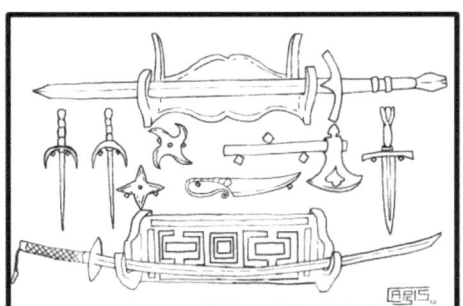
05 - "Blade"

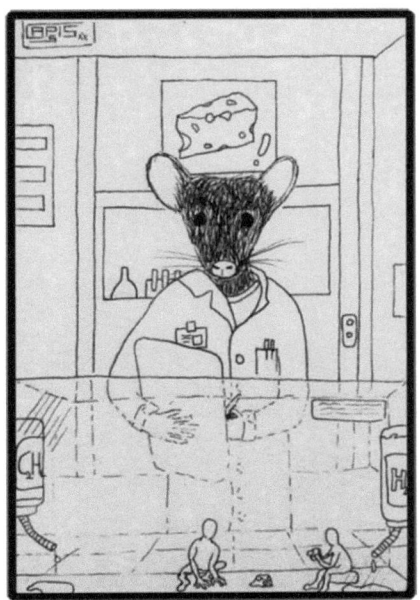
06 - "Rodent"

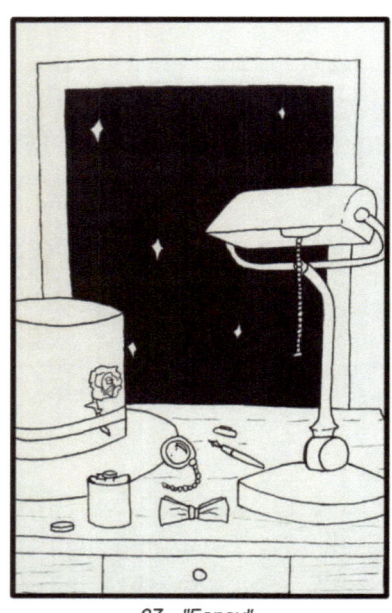
07 - "Fancy"

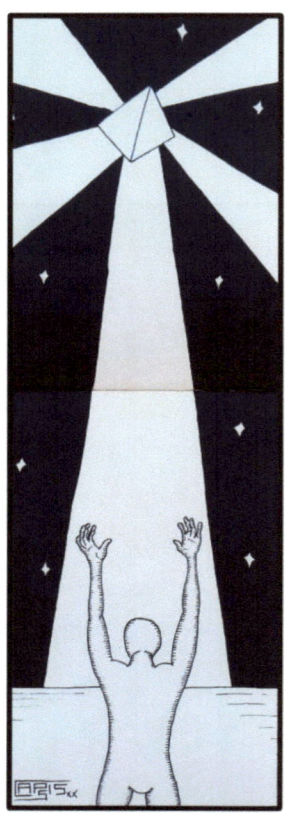
09 - "Throw"

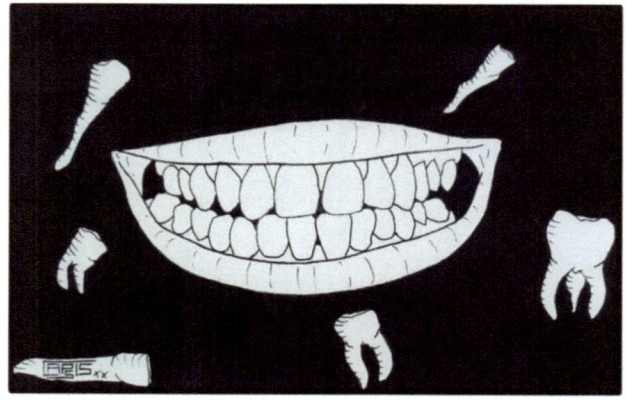
08 - "Teeth"

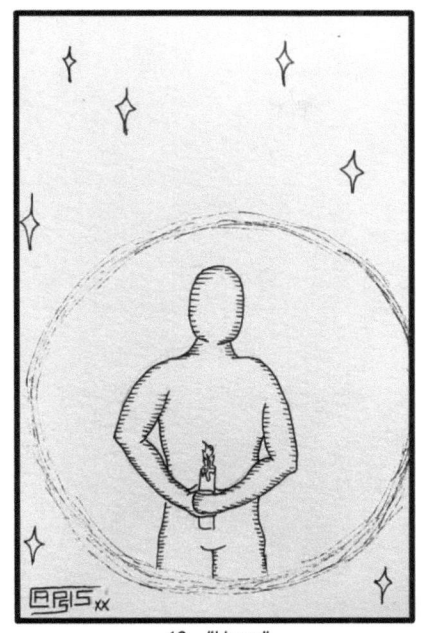
10 - "Hope"

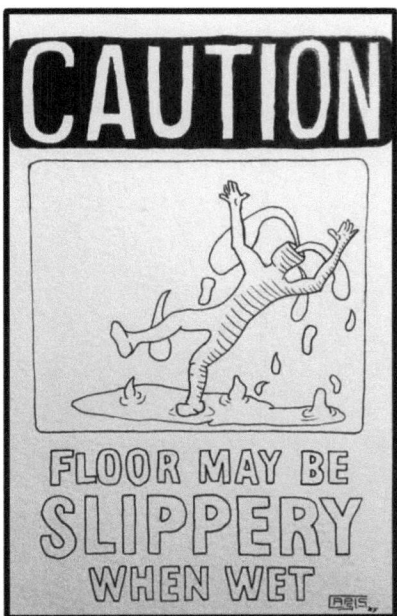
12 - "Slippery"

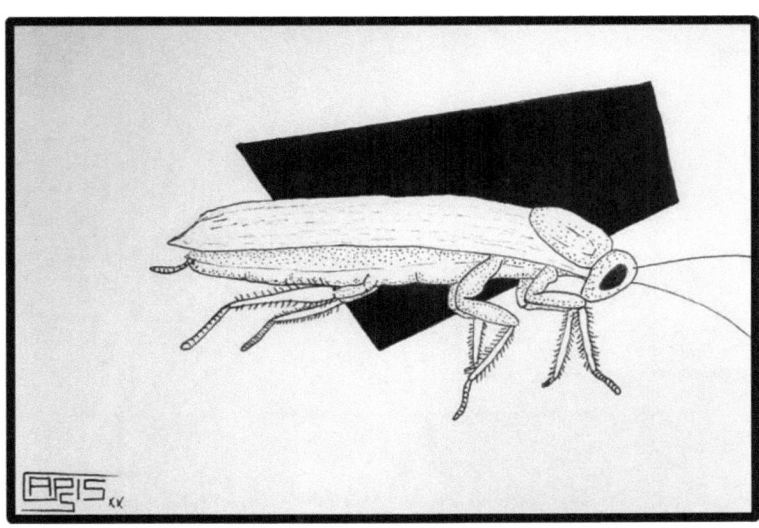
11 - "Disgusting"

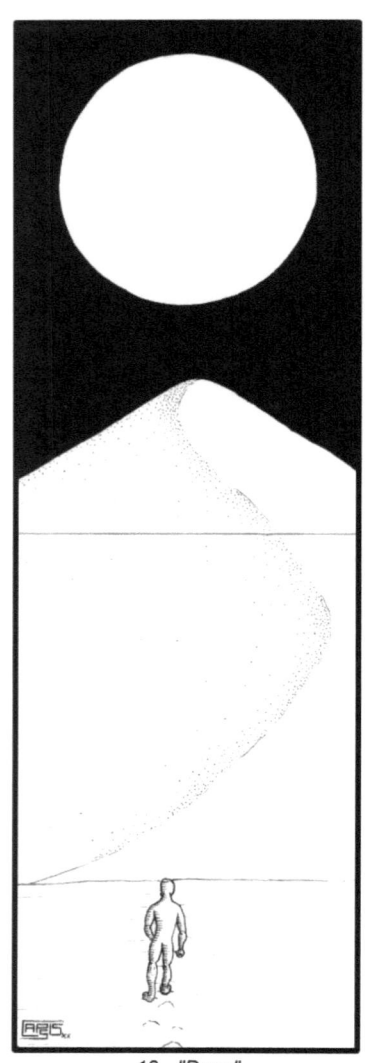
13 - "Dune"

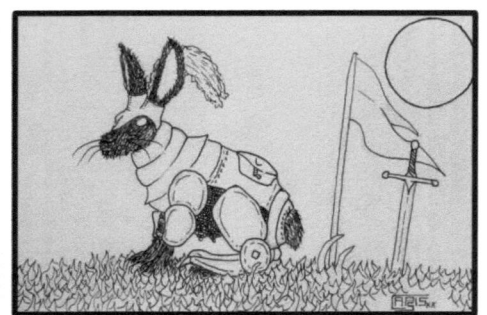
14 - "Armor"

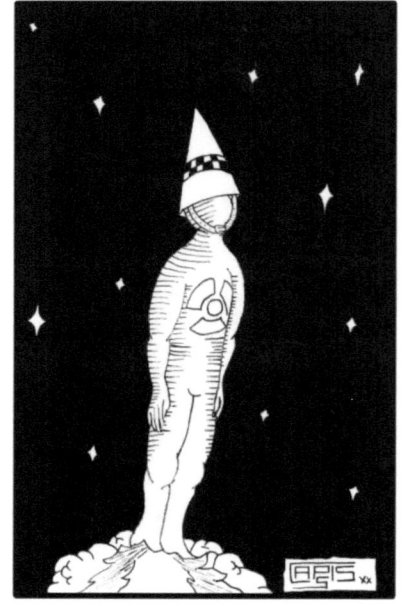
16 - "Rocket"

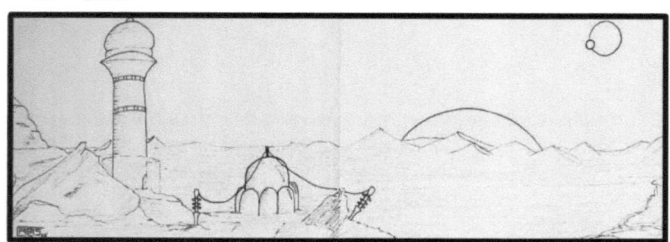
15 - "Outpost"

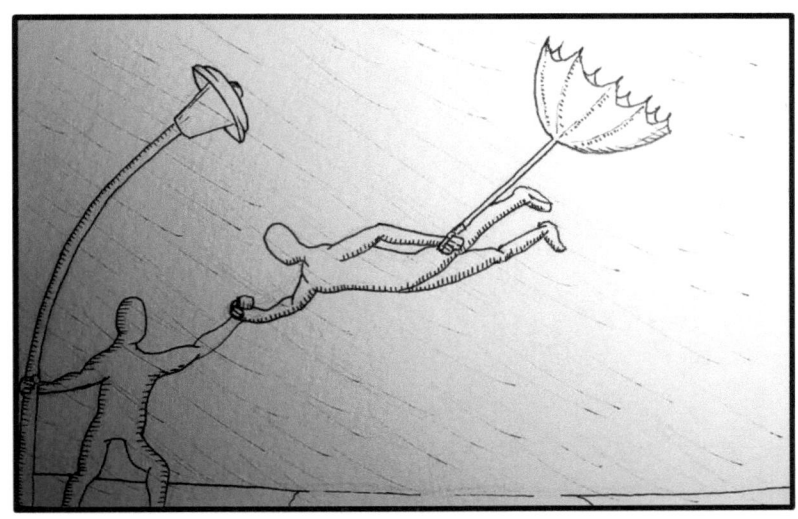
17 - "Storm"

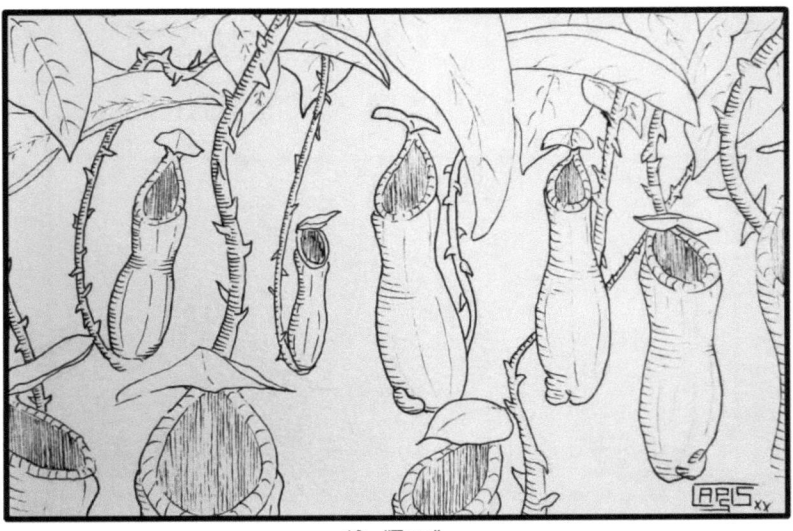
18 - "Trap"

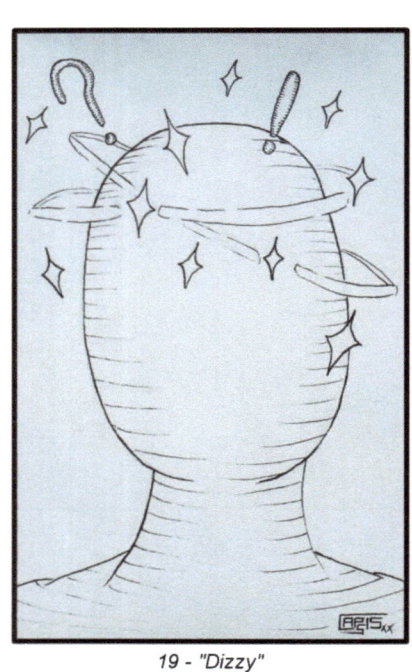
19 - "Dizzy"

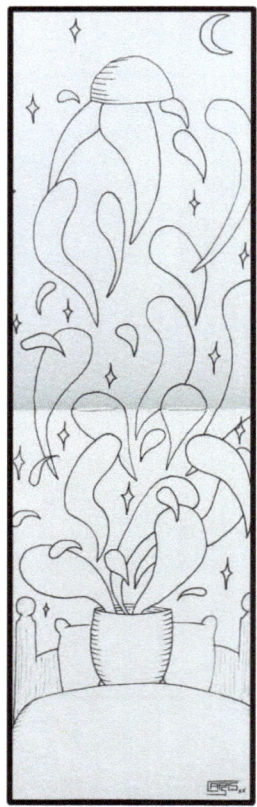
21 - "Sleep"

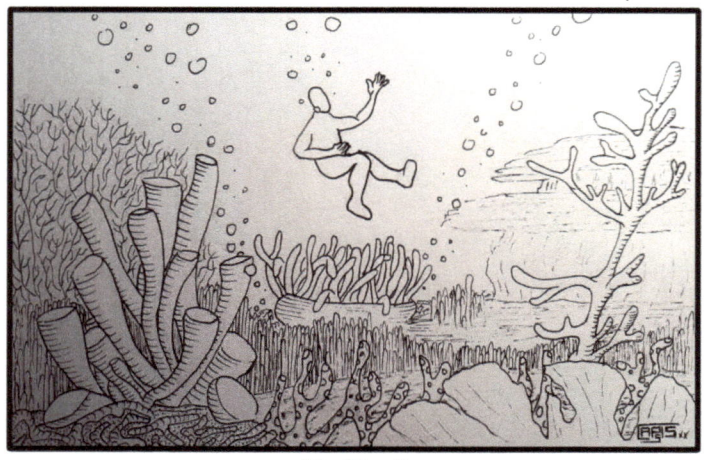
20 - "Coral"

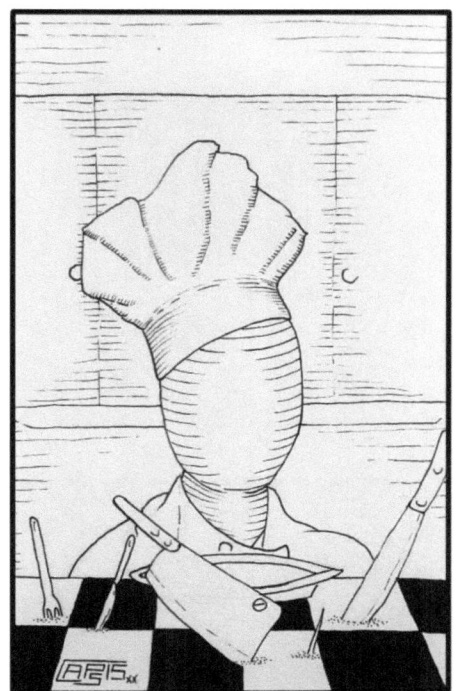

22 - "Chef"

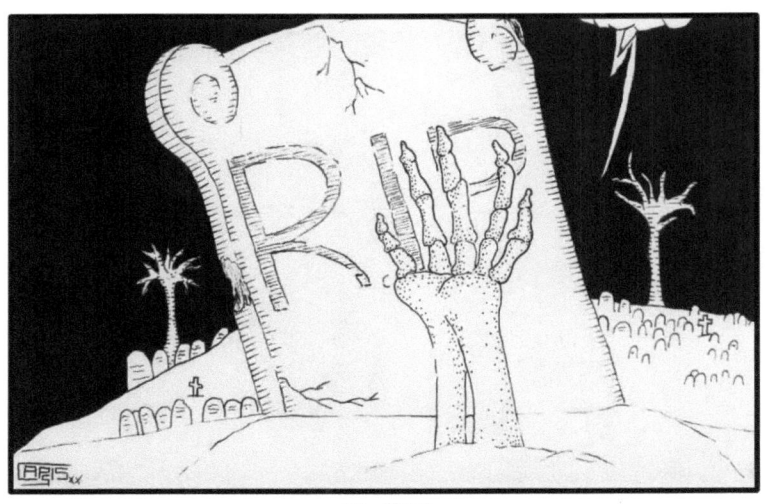

23 - "Rip"

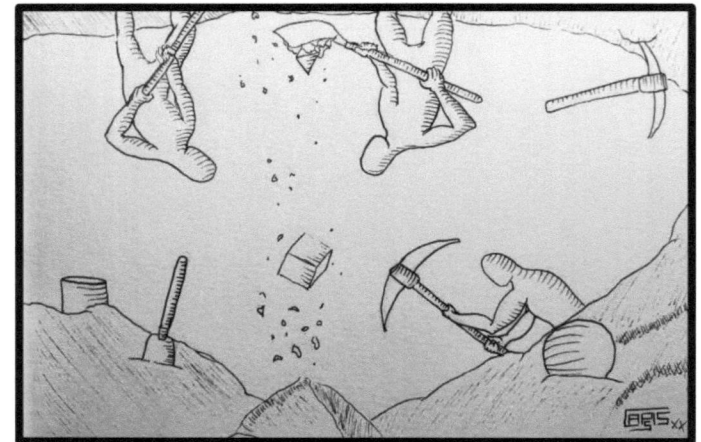

24 - "Dig"

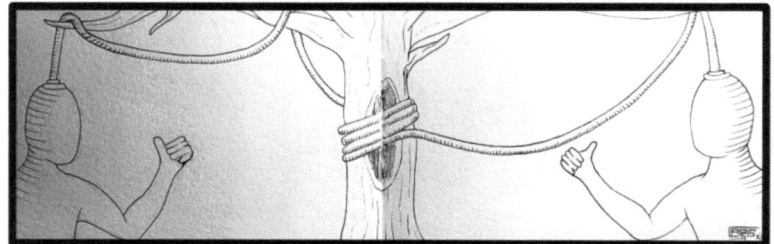

25 - "Buddy"

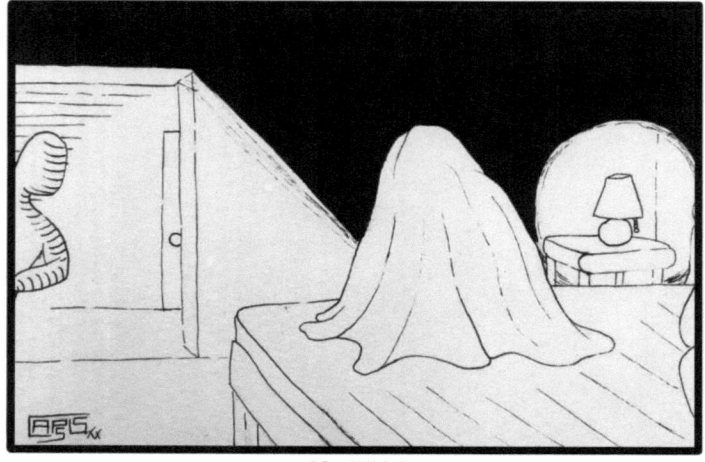

26 - "Hide"

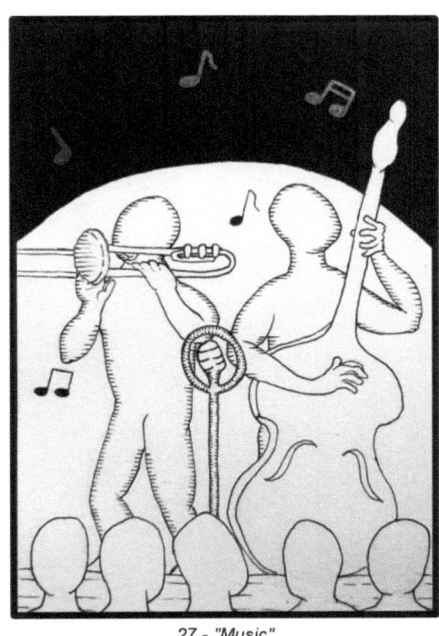
27 - "Music"

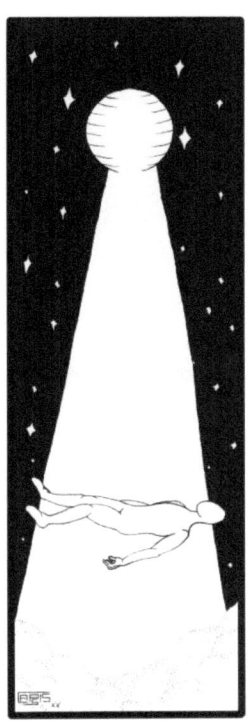
28 - "Float"

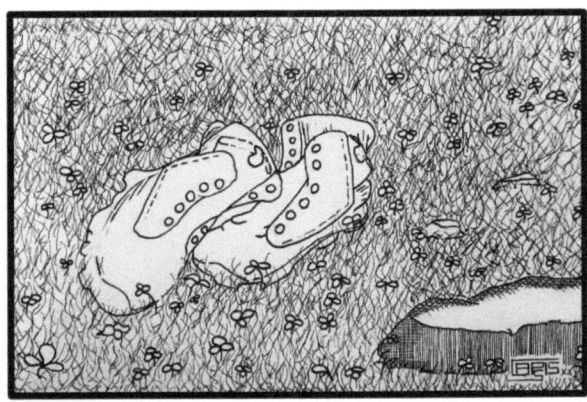
29 - "Shoes"

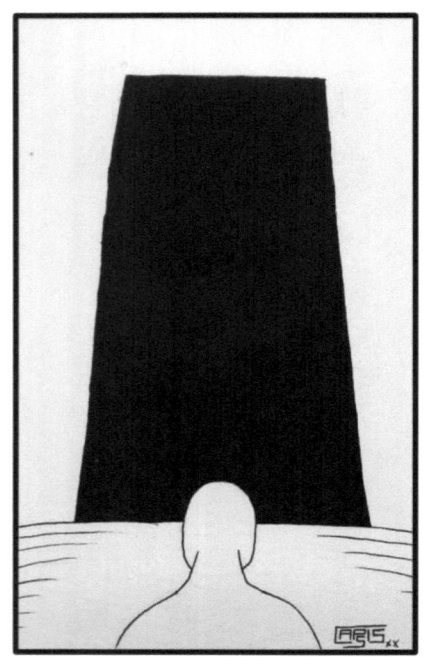

30 - "Ominous"

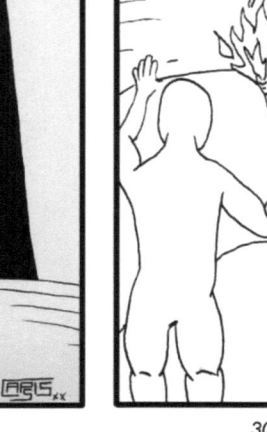

30B - "Ominous"
(Alternative design, I never used)

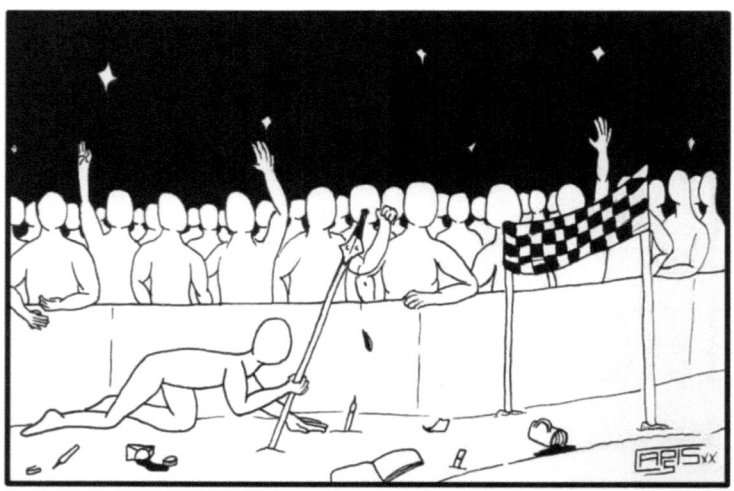

31 - "Crawl"

No matter what challenges you'll face.
Whether it's in life or art:
Just start, go with it and see where you end up.
That's what I did and I am quite happy with the result!

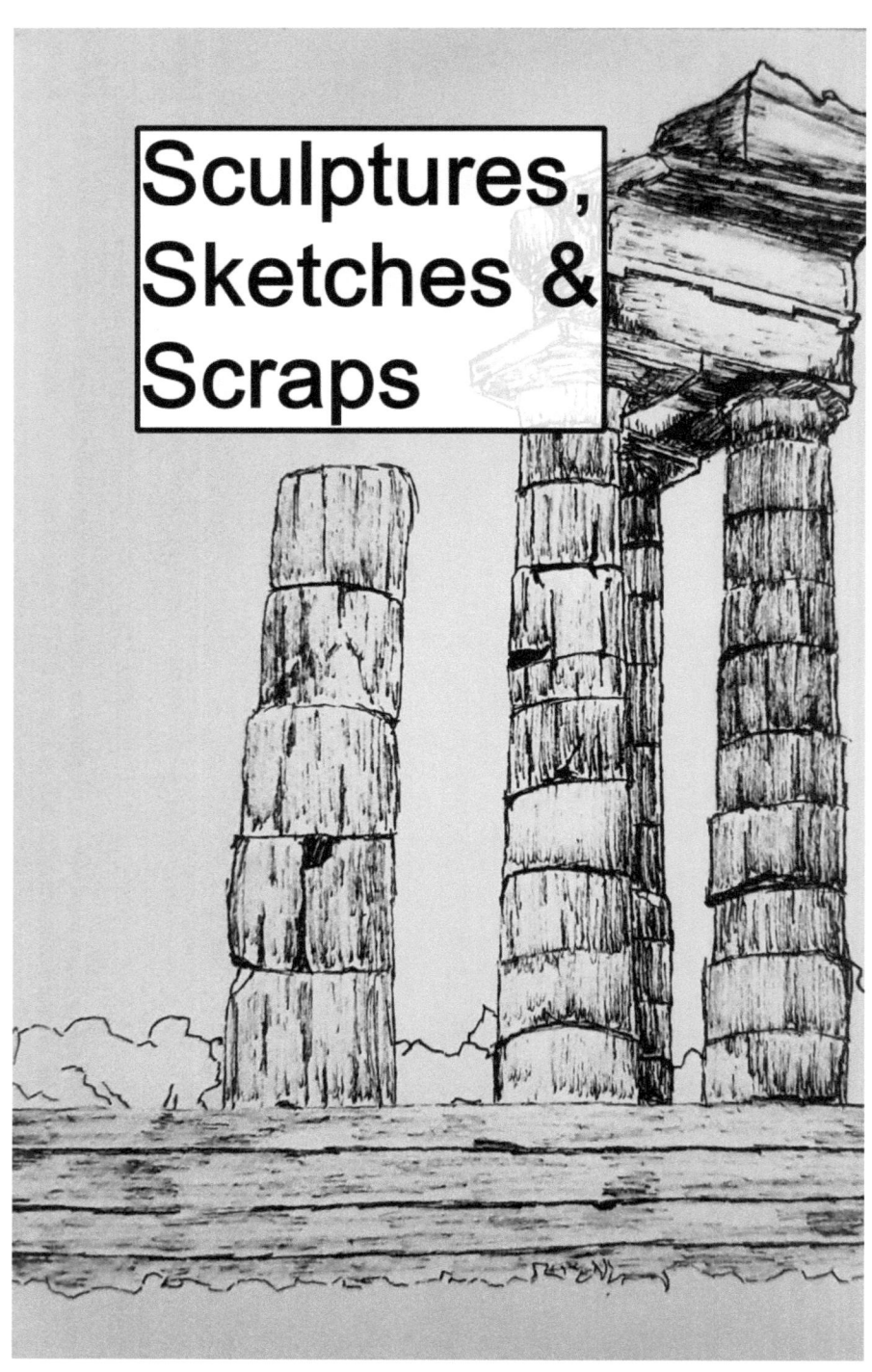

Sculptures, Sketches & Scraps

This final chapter starts with my first pencil drawings of 2020 (all of them feature my Initials "JL" as a signature). I created them somewhat naively, before figuring out that working with other mediums was a possibility. In the end you could say that I found my favorite artistic tool in ink, but it all started here. Even if these pieces seem to be a bit amateurish (at least that's what I think of it now), they mark an important milestone in my journey. Without these everything that you've seen up to this point would not exist.
Also I figured that the few sculptures I conceived would find their place in here, along with the illustrations that did not fit into any of the other chapters.
Anyway there are a lot of surprises waiting for you on the next pages, so let's dive right in.

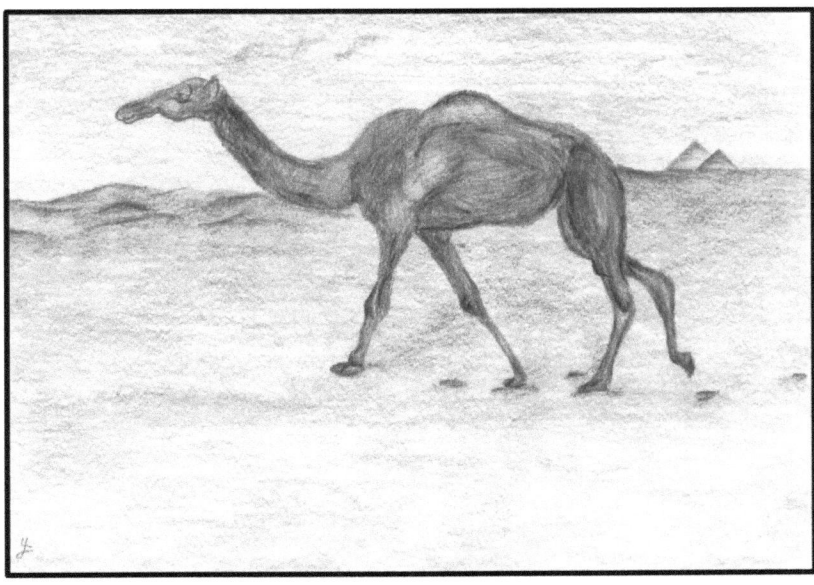

"Camel" - Pencil sketch

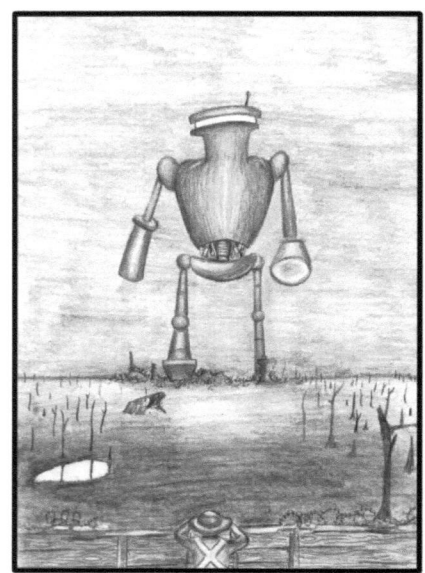
"Colossus" - Pencil sketch

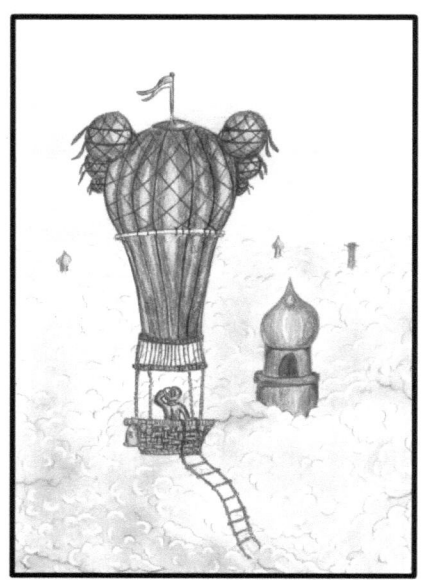
"Journey to the city of spires"

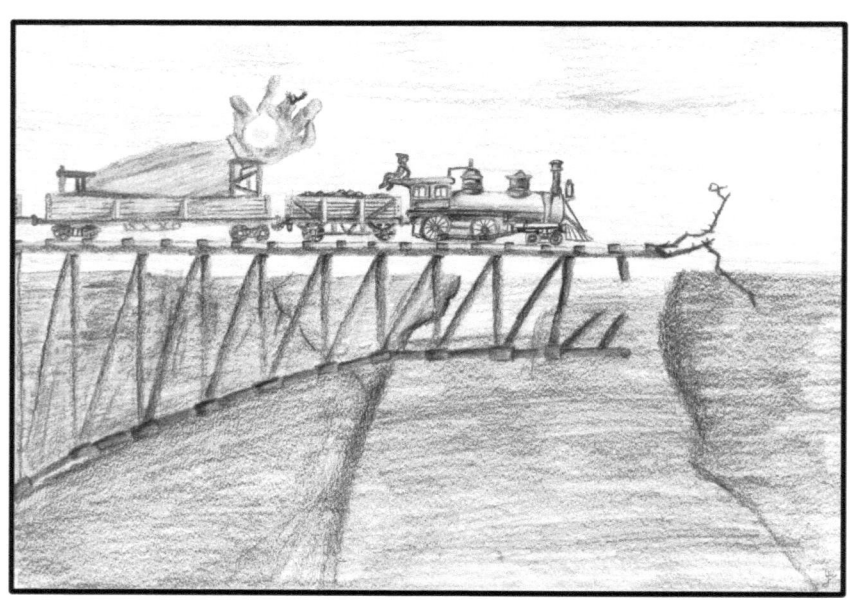
"Railroad Journey" - Pencil sketch

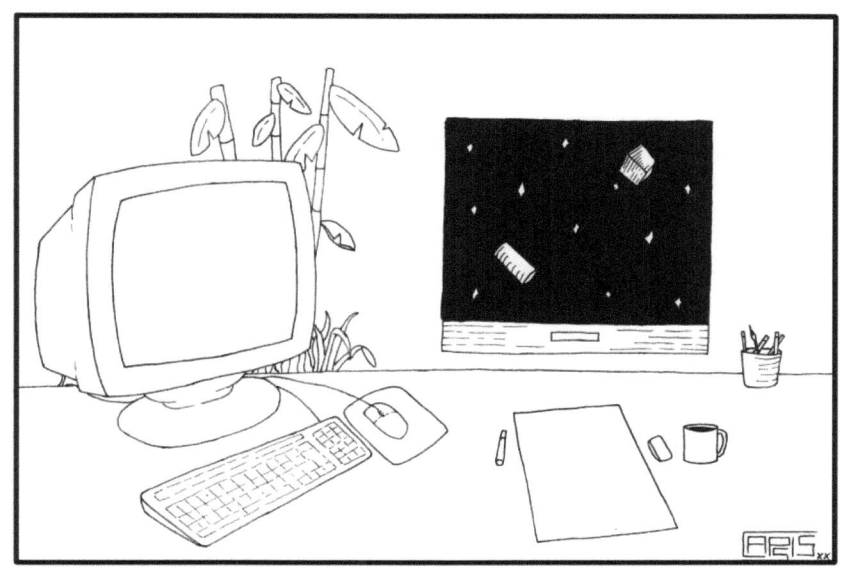

"Workspace" - Ink on paper

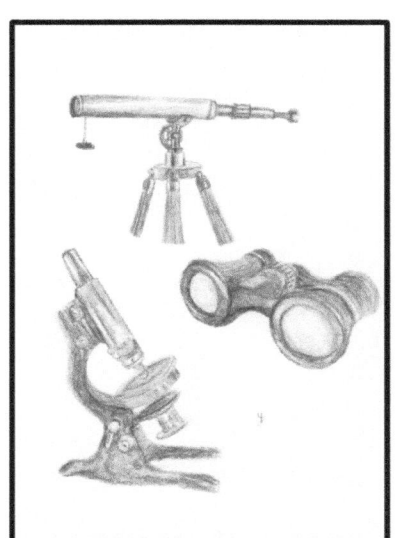

"Occular devices" - Pencil sketch

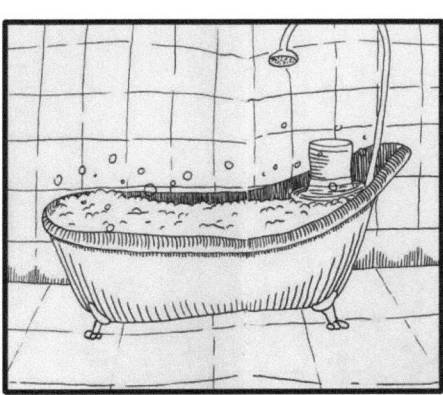

"Bathtub" - Ink on paper

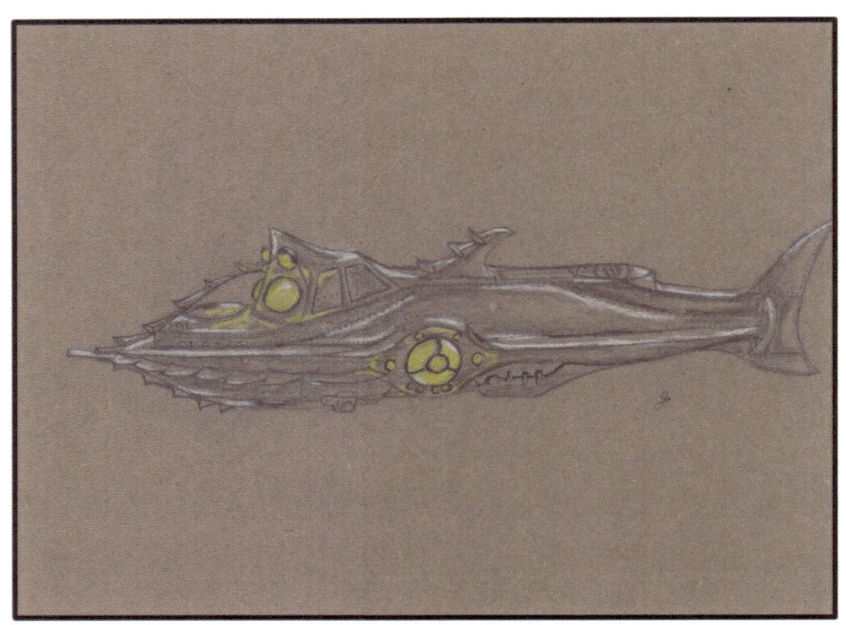
"The Nautilus" - Various pencils on toned paper

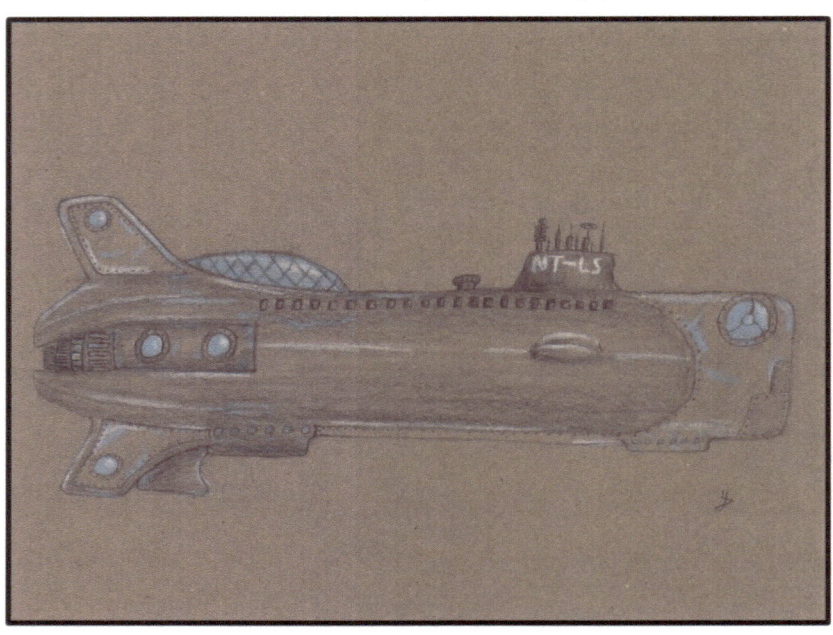
"The Nautilus (Reimagining)" - Various pencils on toned paper

Animals

I don't really know why but I drew a lot of animals throughout the year...

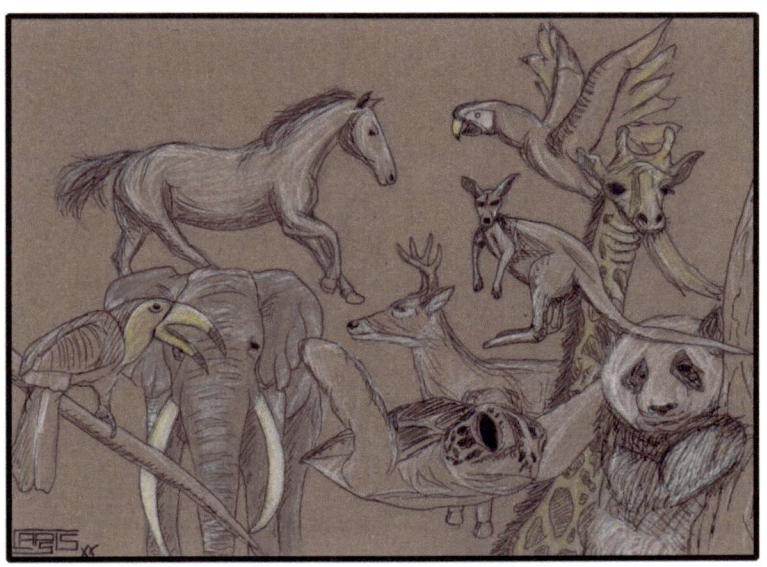

"Animals" - Ink & various pencils on toned paper

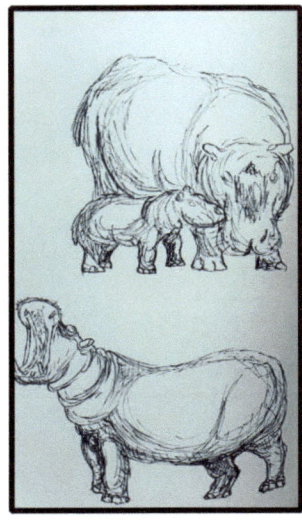

"Hippos" - Ink on paper

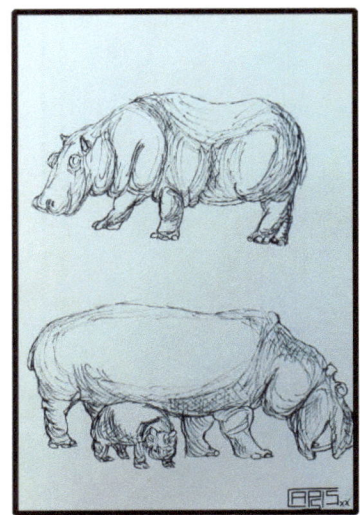

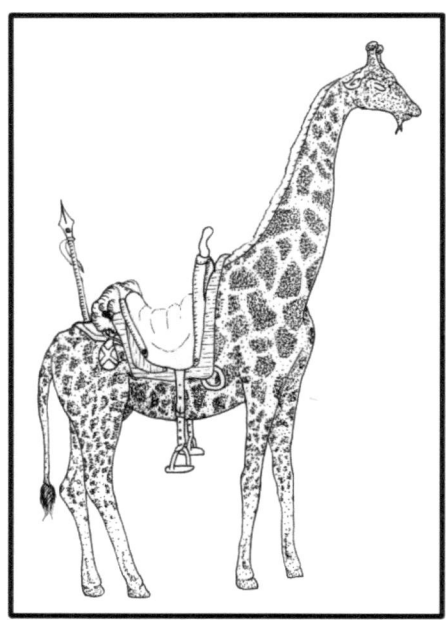
"Giraffe" - Ink on paper

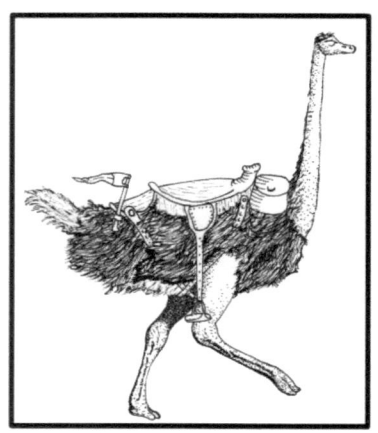
"Ostrich" - Ink on paper

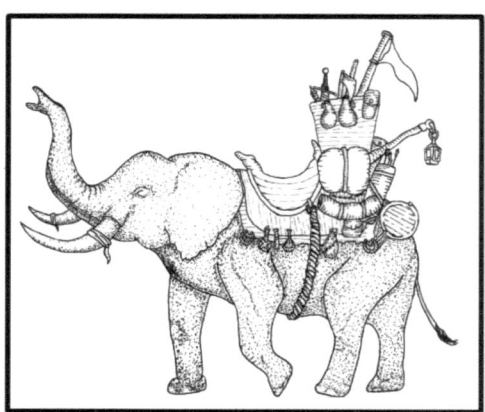
"Elephant" - Ink on paper

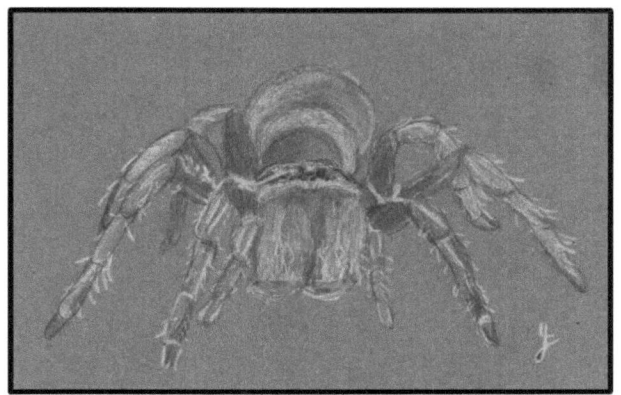
"Spider" - Pencils on toned paper

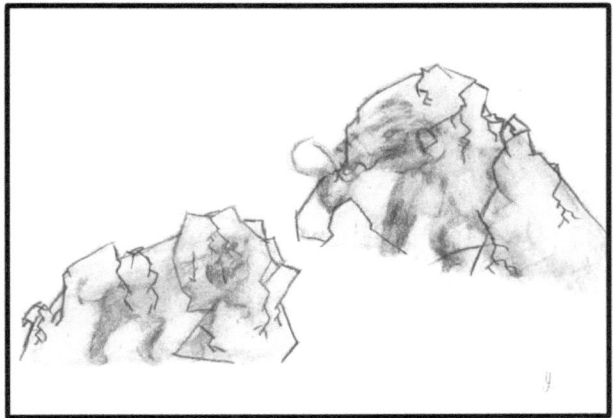
"Animals frozen in ice" - Pencil sketch

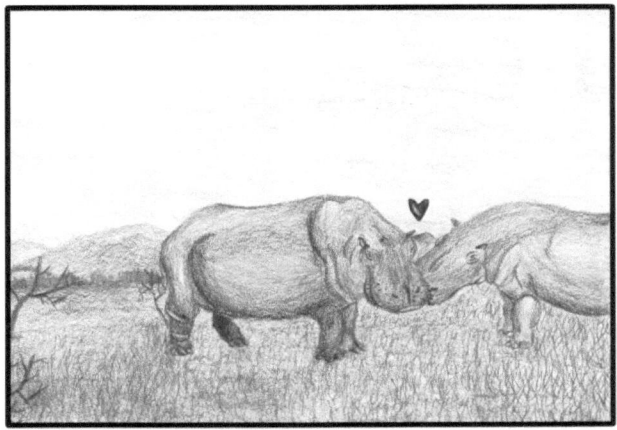
"Hippos on Valentines" - Pencil sketch

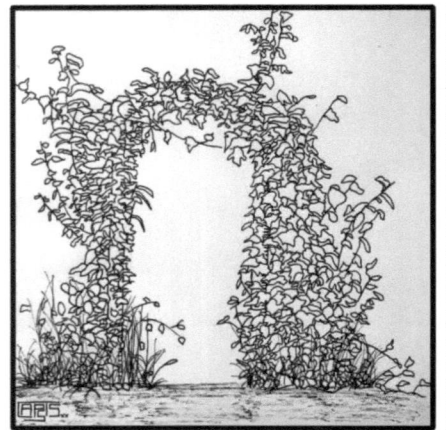
"Overgrown" - Ink on paper

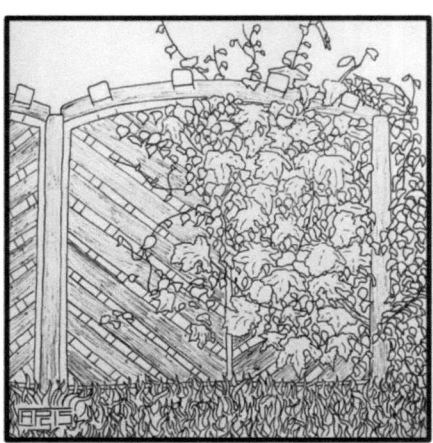
"Overgrown II" - Ink on paper

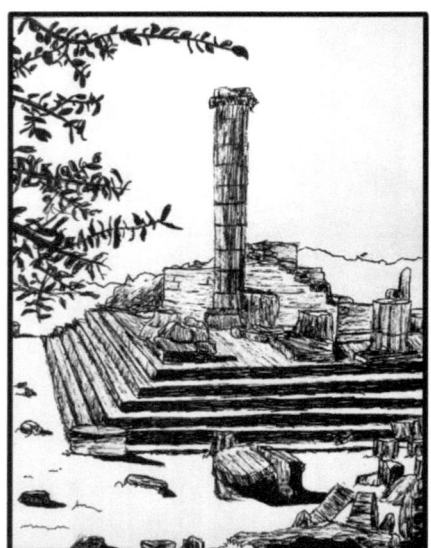
"Ruins" - Ink on paper

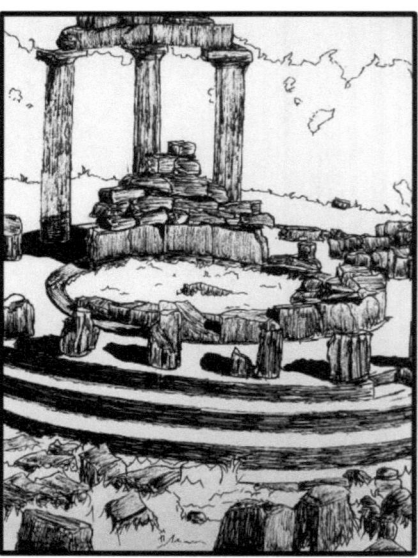
"Temple of the oracle of Delphi"
- Ink on paper

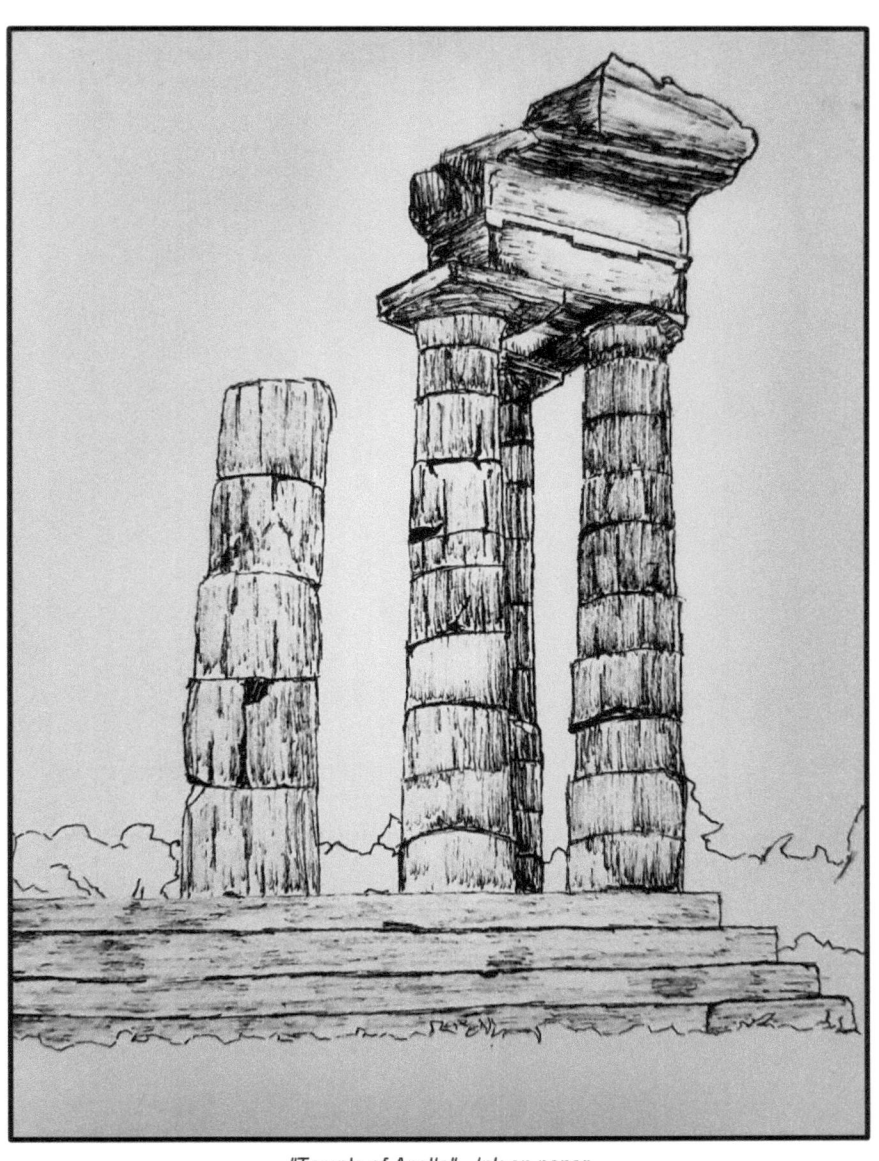

"Temple of Apollo" - Ink on paper

Sketching People

Drawing people is the next step up from drawing animals. At least in my opinion. Here are my first sketches of people in different poses and situations.
The art I'm doing today is often based on people or individuals, so I think these were some kind of starting point for me.

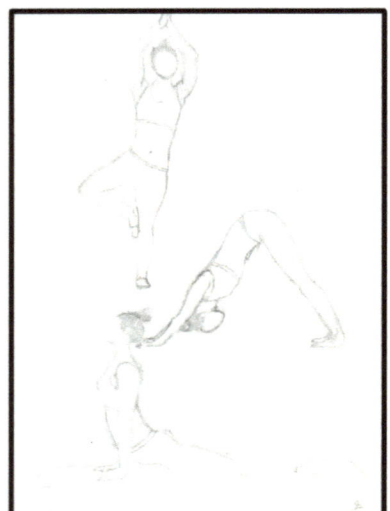
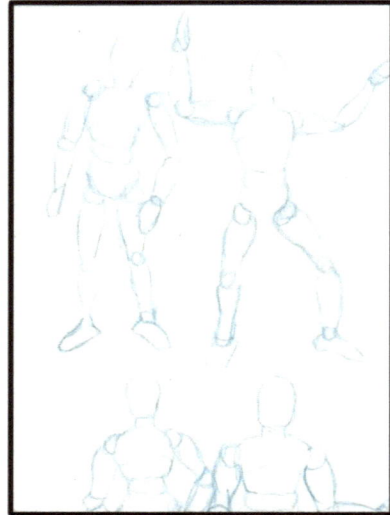
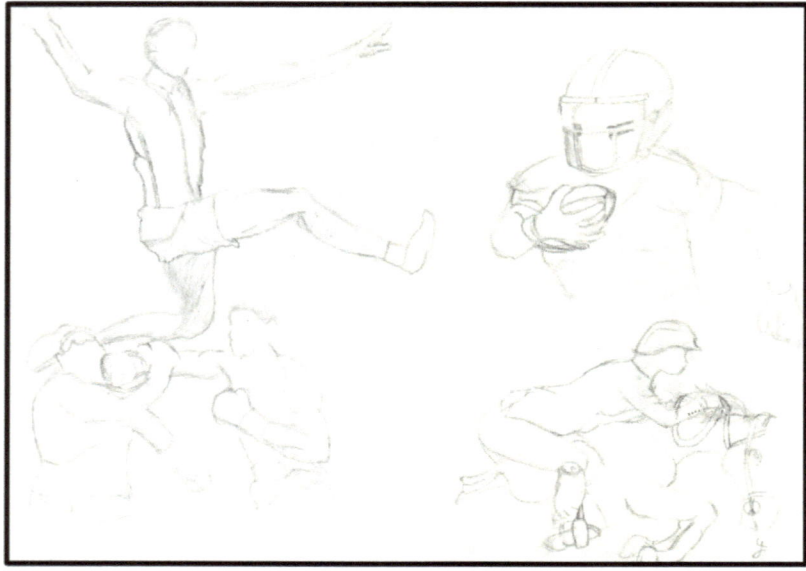

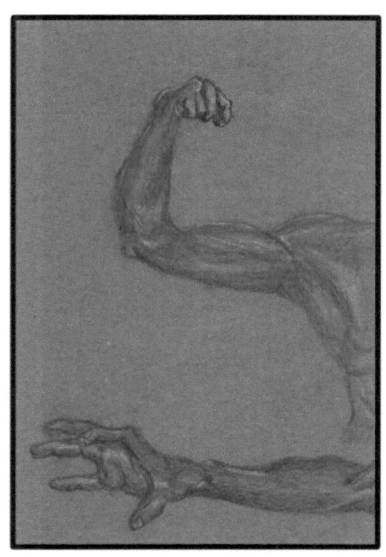 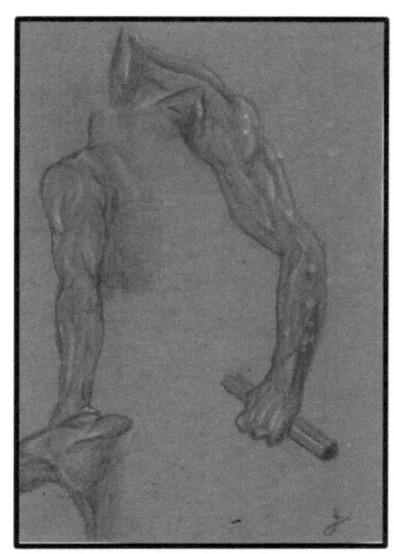

Arms

I created these sketches (various pencils on toned paper) in preparation for my first sculpture of an arm (Pictures on the next page).
On the upper right you can even see some droplets of clay on the paper. Sculpting can be very messy and I used these as reference throughout my process.

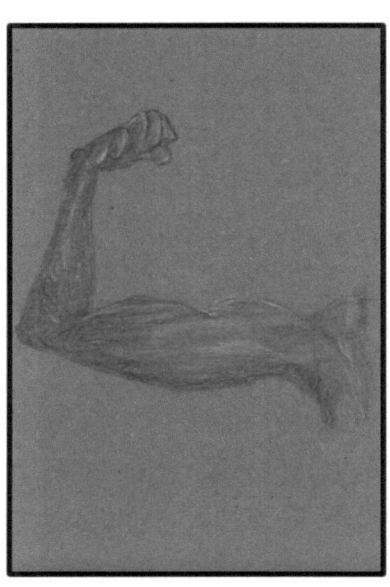 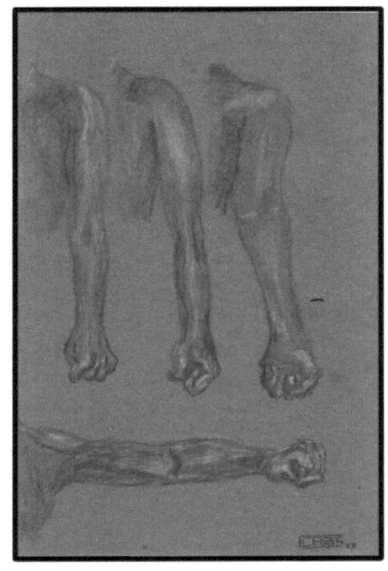

Sculptures

There are worlds between making a sculpture and drawing on a two dimensional surface. I had to think about using my hands and tools in a way that was completely new for me. Nevertheless you can equally create something from nothing. The end result is even more impressing when you can touch the object you created from a once formless mass of clay.

I had a lot of fun working on these but at the same time I feel like I could have done more. My main focus will probably always remain on drawing but I'm sure that I'll make more sculptures in the future. I've already learned a lot about sculpting from these few attempts but there is always room for improvement.

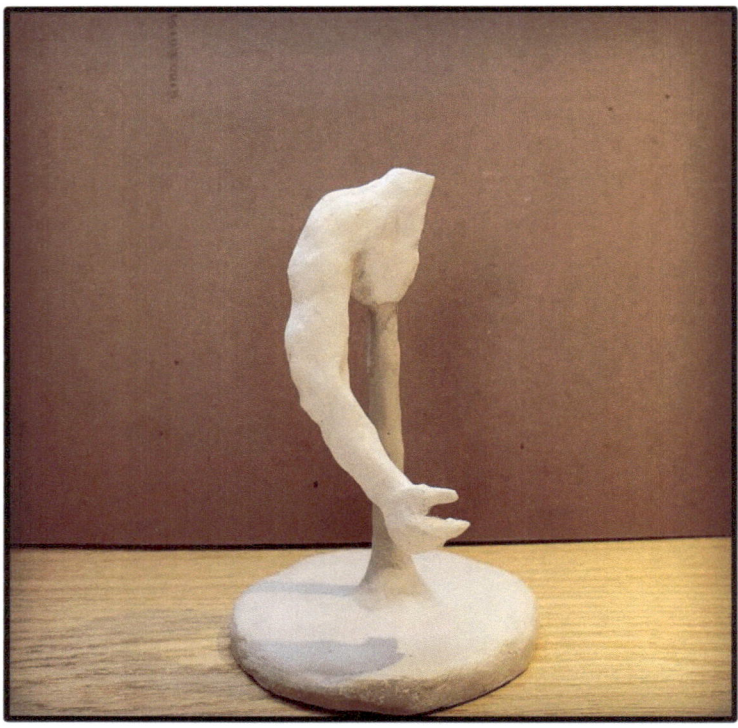

"Arm" - Clay sculpture

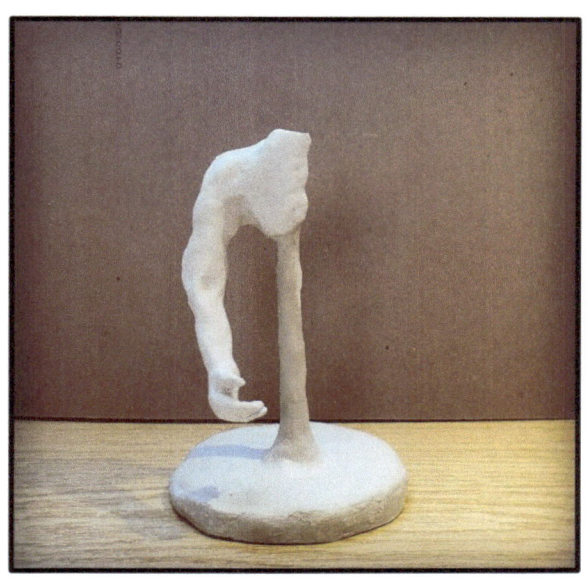

"Arm" - Clay sculpture
(different perspective)

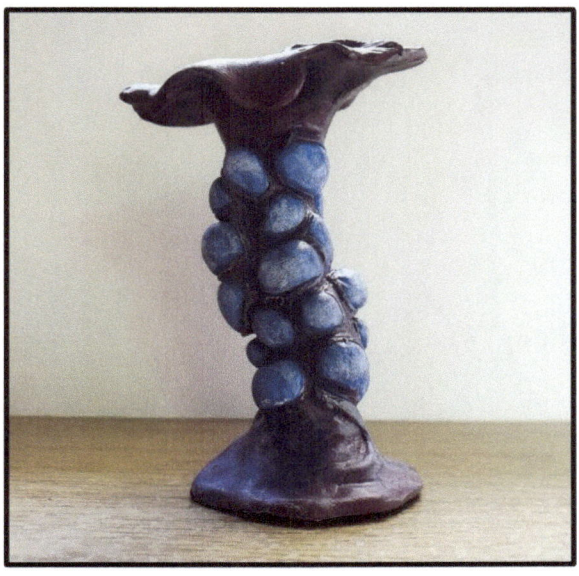

"Unnamed sculpture" - Polymer clay painted with acrylic colors

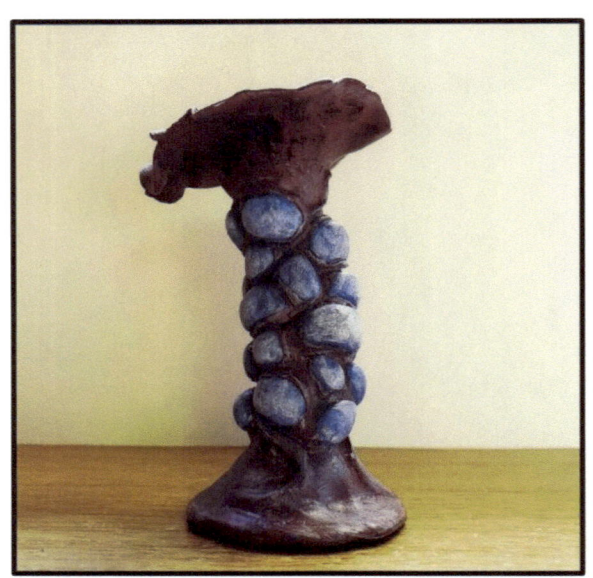

*"Unnamed sculpture" - Polymer clay
(different perspective)*

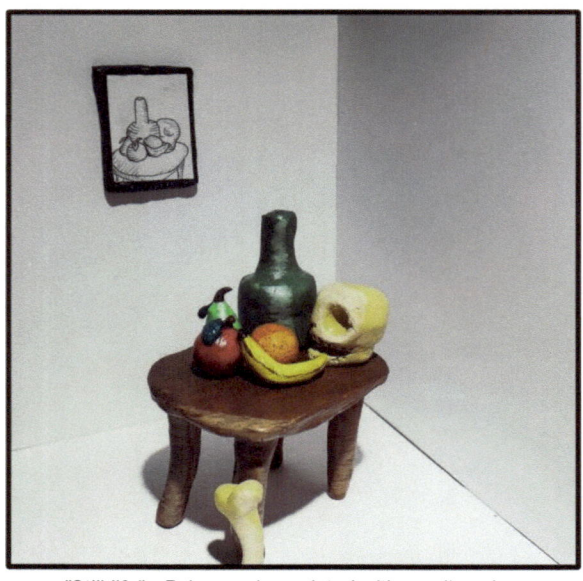

*"Still life" - Polymer clay painted with acrylic colors
(also ink on paper)*

My Thoughts on sculpting

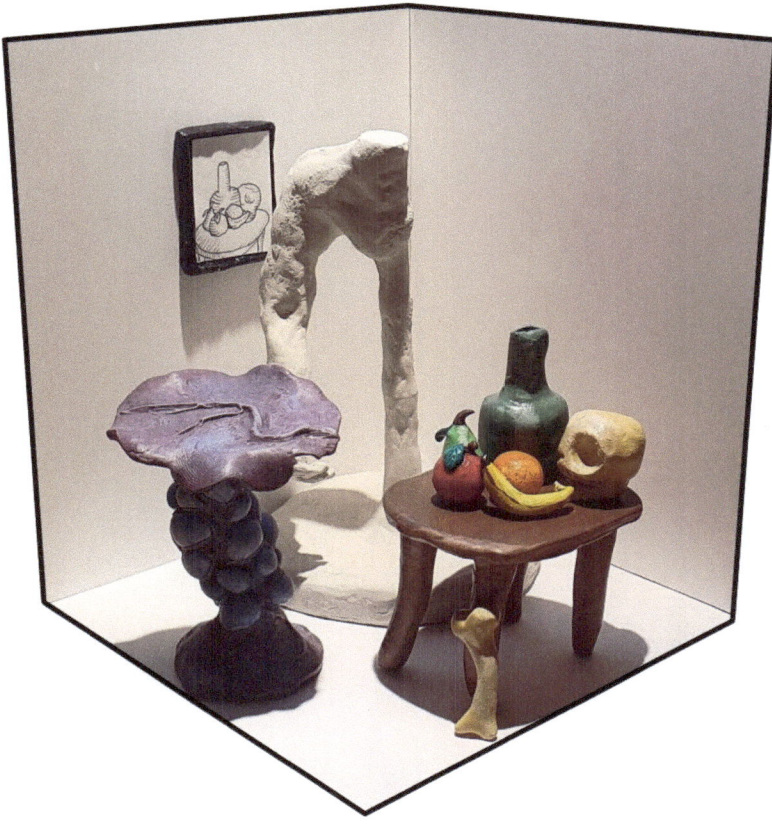

I can only emphasize this again. Sculpting is something special to me. Maybe even more so than drawing, painting or illustrating.
Creating something literally with your own hands and then seeing the result is truly awe inspiring. Maybe I'm exaggerating though. After all, I only did three sculptures this year.
However I'm sure that there will be many more in 2021. I can only propose to anyone who reads this to try and create your own sculpture. When you're done, I'm sure you will understand my enthusiasm for this form of art.

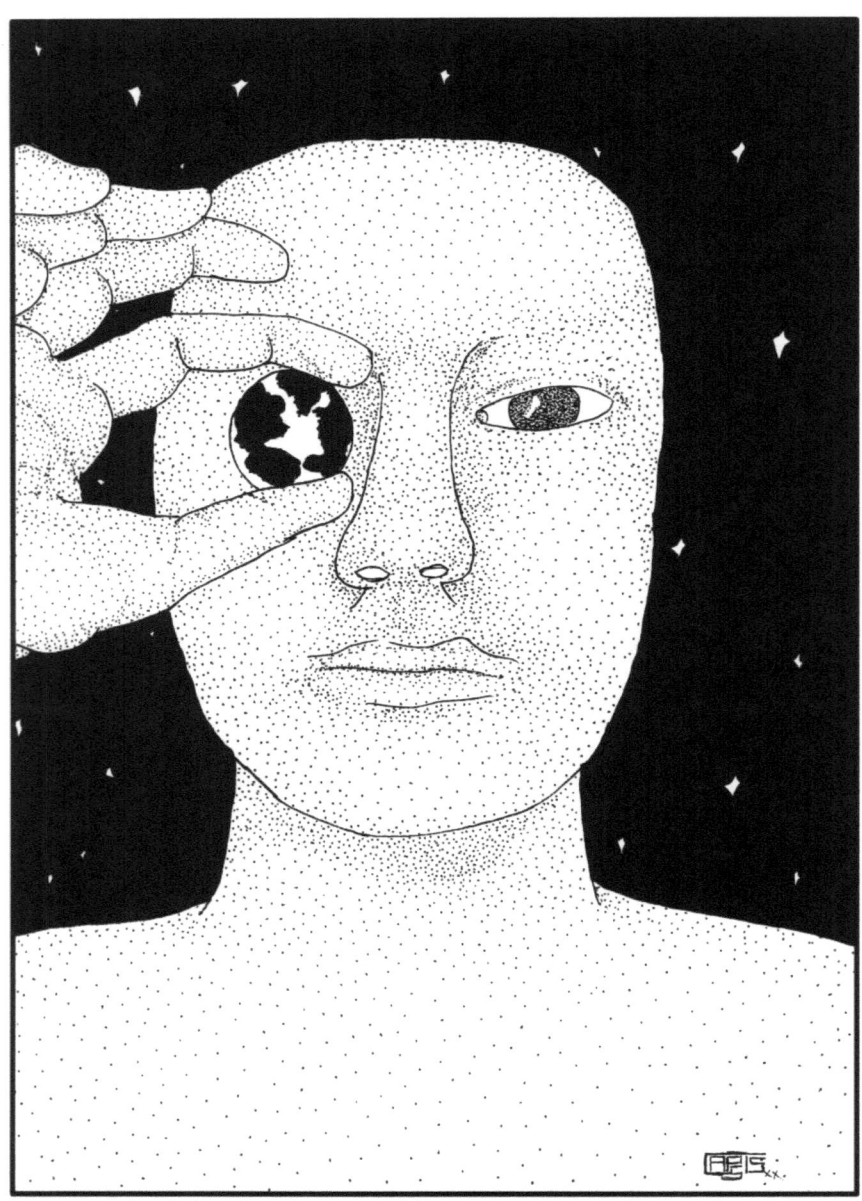
"Self portrait towards the beginning of the year"

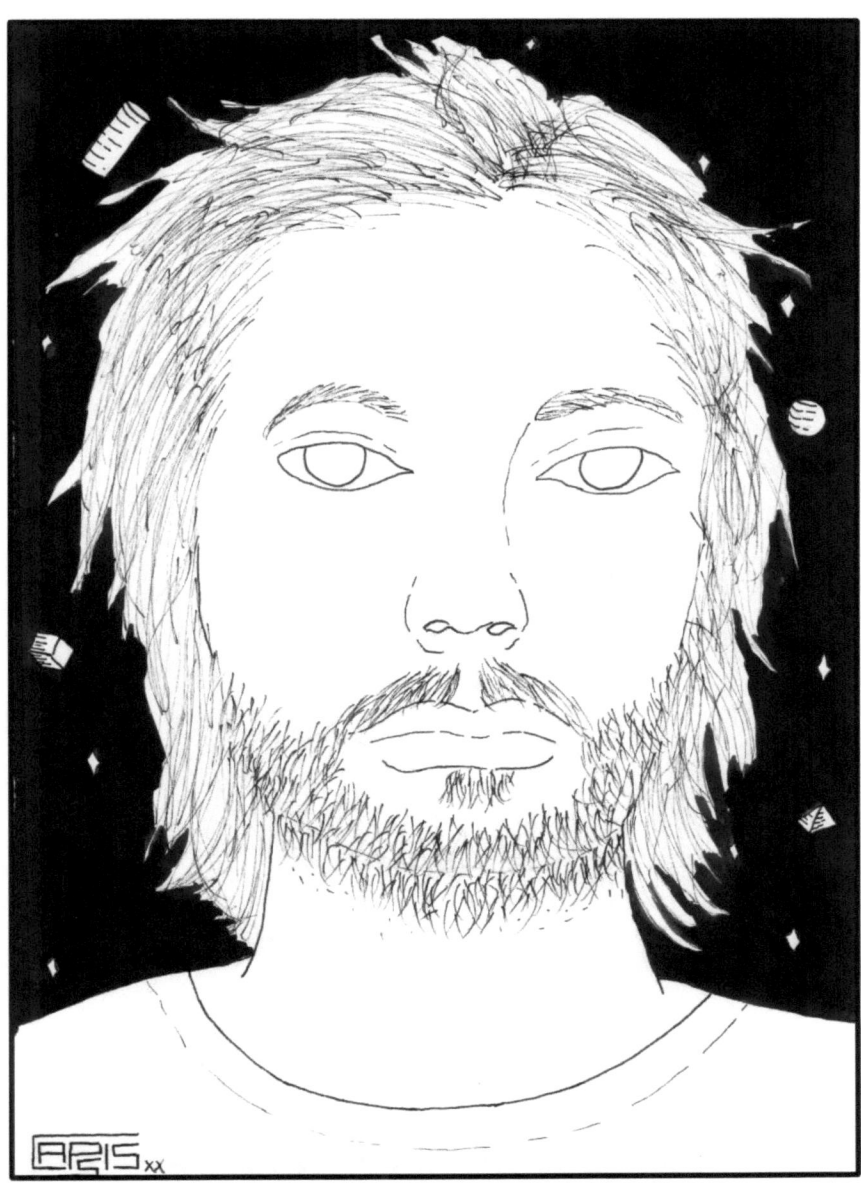
"Self portrait towards the end of the year"

The Future

What lies in the future for any of us? No one can tell, including me. Will I continue creating art? If I am able to then yes, definitely. Am I working on any new big projects? Constantly, of course. If everything goes according to my plan I'll be releasing a few more books in 2021. As 2020 showed, you can never know how crazy things will get so fingers crossed.

Still, I hope that I'll be able to create and publish more of my art throughout the year in any way, shape or form.

Below this text is my first real illustration of 2021 as a little preview for what is yet to come.

Anyway that's it for 2020. I sincerely hope that you found something interesting here. If you did I'd be happy if you join me on any of my social media sites to accompany me on my artistic journey. I'm already excited to see what will happen next!

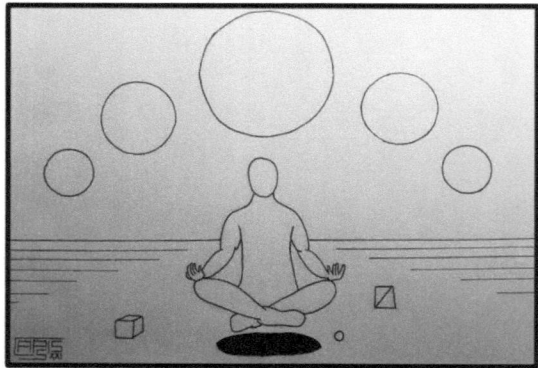

"Meditation (Day)" - Ink on paper

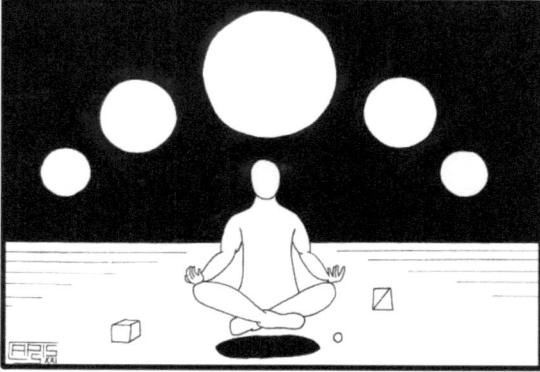

"Meditation (Night)" - Ink on paper

www.ingramcontent.com/pod-product-compliance
Lightning Source LLC
Chambersburg PA
CBHW040232220526
45473CB00001B/210